MYTHBUSTING
HEMINGWAY

MYTHBUSTING HEMINGWAY

Debunking Hemingway Myths and
Celebrating the Extraordinary Stories of His Life

Thomas Bevilacqua and Robert K. Elder

LYONS
PRESS

Essex, Connecticut

An imprint of Globe Pequot, the trade division of The Rowman & Littlefield
Publishing Group, Inc.
4501 Forbes Blvd., Ste. 200
Lanham, MD 20706
www.rowman.com

Distributed by NATIONAL BOOK NETWORK

British Library Cataloguing in Publication Information available

Library of Congress Cataloging-in-Publication Data

Names: Bevilacqua, Thomas, author. | Elder, Robert K., author.
Title: Mythbusting Hemingway : debunking Hemingway myths and
    celebrating the extraordinary stories of his life / Thomas Bevilacqua and
    Robert K. Elder.
Description: Essex, Connecticut : Lyons Press, [2023] | Includes
    bibliographical references.
Identifiers: LCCN 2023017853 (print) | LCCN 2023017854 (ebook) | ISBN
    9781493064052 (paperback) | ISBN 9781493080618 (epub)
Subjects: LCSH: Hemingway, Ernest, 1899-1961—Miscellanea.
Classification: LCC PS3515.E37 Z582485 2023 (print) | LCC PS3515.E37
    (ebook) | DDC 813/.52—dc23/eng/20230620
LC record available at https://lccn.loc.gov/2023017853
LC ebook record available at https://lccn.loc.gov/2023017854

CONTENTS

CONTENTS

Hemingway

The Legend and the Life

Robert K. Elder

The idea for this book hit me while lounging poolside at Ernest Hemingway's house in Key West.

OK, not actually *lounging*, but I was sitting there, dodging the hot sun, for hours, talking to tourists and signing copies of *Hidden Hemingway: Inside the Ernest Hemingway Archives of Oak Park*, a book I'd written with friends Mark Cirino and Aaron Vetch. I was by the pool because the bookstore on the grounds is much too small for a signing event, so the (very kind) staff set me up with a table outside in the shade.

While there, I heard docent after docent tell the story about "Hemingway's last penny," a shiny 1934 wheat penny embedded near the pool. The core of the story was that, when Hemingway returned from a trip, he'd found an extravagant pool installed by his second wife, Pauline.

"Here," he scolded, "You might as well have my last penny too!" To add a spiteful permanence to the insult, he had the penny embedded next to the pool.

And I heard each tour guide tell this story, with different intensity and, sometimes, completely different sets of contradictory facts. It didn't make a ton of sense, either, given that the house was a gift from Pauline's uncle, and they lived largely off her fortune.

"Shouldn't people know the actual story?" I asked the museum manager.

"I like that everyone has their own spin on the story," he said, and he changed the subject.

And when I asked local Key West and Hemingway historian Brewster Chamberlin about the penny, he simply said, "I wish people would stop telling that story. It's not true."

So we sort that myth out on page 152.

So many Hemingway myths, misquotes, and flat-out fabrications out there not only ignore the scholarship but also obscure the truly extraordinary things that Hemingway did and said.

But if you cobbled together a biography from internet sources, even some reputable ones, you might read something like this: Hemingway was wounded as a soldier in World War I. He sparked an entire literary movement and wrote the famous six-word short story "For Sale: Baby Shoes, Never Worn." During World War II, Hemingway killed 122 Nazis while embedded with the Twenty-Second Infantry. He was an art collector who loved the works of Cézanne and Monet—and even owned a painting by Joan Miró. And he offered memorable advice for both writing and living, including "Write drunk; edit sober" and "We are all broken. That's how the light gets in."

Only one of the above statements is true, however. He really was an avid art collector who owned Joan Miró's painting *The Farm*.

The problem is, Hemingway's legendary life sparked legends and myths of its own. Blame misinformation or the internet, but the fact is, Hemingway fell victim to that famous line from John Ford's *The Man Who Shot Liberty Valance*: "When the legend becomes fact, print the legend."

Even Hemingway's publisher was printing myths during the author's lifetime.

In October 1940, Hemingway's new novel, *For Whom the Bell Tolls*, was featured in the Book-of-the-Month Club's magazine. The magazine includes an essay featuring the byline of his editor, Max Perkins, who promises to dispel a bunch of falsehoods about Hemingway but spreads a few more.

The piece begins, "In spite of Ernest Hemingway's repugnance to publicity—his first and most emphatic request to his publishers was that nothing about his personal life be given out—he is one of those about whom legends gather; and since he is disinclined to talk about himself it is hard to disentangle truth from rumor."

Perkins then adds hyperbole to Hemingway's boxing training and war experiences, and he says that the author left home before the age of sixteen (blatantly untrue), which further tangled truth and rumor.

It wasn't all victimhood, mind you; Hemingway had a hand in adding misinformation to his own biography. For example, in the 1935 essay for *Esquire* magazine titled "Remembering Shooting-Flying: A Key West Letter," he wrote that "the house where I was born was gone and they had cut down the oak trees." But all three of the homes he lived in, here in Oak Park, Illinois, are still standing, including his birthplace (now Ernest Hemingway's Birthplace Home Museum). He also exaggerated his activity during World War I (and World War II), and he could be hyperbolic about his love life.

But too many people have been printing Hemingway's legend—so much so that it obscures the heroic, sad, and truly extraordinary details of his real life.

Using a series of carefully researched chapters, light-hearted side-bars, and historical photos, *Mythbusting Hemingway* seeks to debunk the memes and celebrate the author's life and career properly by stripping out falsehoods. This book is not just a survey of existing scholarship; it also contributes new research to the field. This book acts as a repository for some of the Hemingway detective work I've done over the past decade as well as significant contributions and collaborations with my friend and previously mentioned coauthor Cirino and a gargantuan amount of work from the coeditor of this book, Thomas Bevilacqua.

Over these past few years, we've had a chance to dig deep and ask questions big and small about Hemingway's life, work, and legacy. But we've also had the opportunity to ask, well, *why*? Why do we care at all? What makes Hemingway such a compelling figure, for all of his obvious, unflattering faults and his massive talent?

Simply put, he was a fascinating figure who lived during historic times. He saw three wars—World War I as an American Red Cross volunteer, and the Spanish Civil War and World War II primarily as a correspondent. He married four strong, captivating women who provided him with support and inspiration. Though born in Oak Park, a suburb of Chicago, Hemingway considered himself a citizen of the world and "a boy with five home towns . . . Paris, Venice, Ketchum (Idaho), Key West and Havana," he wrote Leonard Lyons of the *New York Post* in 1950.

And he was a driven, difficult, and complex person with literary gifts and undeniable charisma. His first wife, Hadley, told Denis Brian for his 1988 book *The True Gen* that Hemingway "was so complicated, so many sides to him, you could hardly make a sketch of him in a geometry book."

But another reason the public remains interested in Hemingway is simple: he has the best-documented human life in the historical record—both his interior and exterior lives. We can rely on his vast professional works as well as the artifacts his family saved from his infanthood. The Hemingway Letters Project will publish six thousand plus letters in a projected seventeen volumes. Plus, new letters—I've found a few of them myself—and new materials fuel fresh scholarship and renewed interest in Hemingway.

But, scholar Verna Kale told me, there's more to it than that: "In reading the incoming letters Hemingway received and going through other people's archives in my research, I've often been struck by how *dull* everyone else is in comparison," Kale said. "People who knew Hemingway talk about his magnetism, and that comes through in his letters. He's just very insightful and funny and was always doing all kinds of neat stuff. You can spend hours with Hemingway's archive without getting bored."

Moreover, *how* we understand him is different. As culture evolves, so does our understanding of him, especially in terms of his interest in gender roles.

"The Hemingway that you know from high school is not the Hemingway we know today," Carl Eby, the president of the Ernest Hemingway Foundation and Society, told me when I interviewed him for the *New York Times* in 2022. "The hyper-machismo was real, but it was less than half the picture. Hemingway's sexuality and gender identity were much more fluid and complex than the general public realizes. The man was a thousand times more interesting and nuanced than the myth would suggest."

With that complexity in mind, and because we know that often Absolute Truth is tough to prove, we've ranked the claims as False, Improbable, Possible, Probable, and True using a Hemingway Truth-o-Meter.

And because new scholarship means new insights, we realize that—gasp!—new information might change or challenge some of the answers in this book. That's how history works. But we've done our best to nail down and annotate all the sources, and when there is disagreement, we've strived to find a scholarly consensus.

It's a fitting treatment for an author who survived back-to-back plane crashes, played the cello, and boxed heavyweight champion Gene Tunney. He was an avid outdoorsman who once shot himself in the leg with a pistol while gaffing a shark. Hemingway was a heavyweight talent who won both the Nobel and Pulitzer Prizes for literature and influenced generations of writers. Oh, and he got into a brawl with Orson Welles.

And all of that is true.

Robert K. Elder
Oak Park, Illinois
2023

"Punctur[ing] the Windbags"

Getting to the Heart of What Matters about Ernest Hemingway

Thomas Bevilacqua

When I think about Ernest Hemingway and the tall tales associated with him, my mind returns to the time in my life when I first critically engaged with the author's work.

Like so many others, my initial entry into Hemingway's writing came in high school with *The Sun Also Rises*. I was swept up in that libertine world of 1920s Paris and Hemingway's stripped-down, no-nonsense prose style that mirrored the toughness of his protagonist, Jake Barnes (and later, as further reading would reveal, Frederic Henry in *A Farewell to Arms*). This created an image—no, a caricature—of Hemingway in my young mind as the model for the literarily inclined man (or boy who wanted to be a man). It loomed large in my thoughts as I traversed different periods in literary history, painted in primary colors and thus lacking in real nuance.

As I began my graduate studies in English, conceiving of myself not just as an enjoyer of literature but also a scholar of it, my eye returned to Hemingway as one whose work I wanted to explore. Here was a chance to build on my enjoyment of his writing and to transform that genuine interest into more scholarly inquiry.

I remember one of my professors during that time in graduate school, Barry Maine at Wake Forest University, making a point that took apart that broad, simplistic image of Hemingway I had in my mind (something that desperately needed to happen).

We were discussing *A Farewell to Arms* in a course on World War I in American literature and visual art. Professor Maine alluded to the fact that people always think they would like to go out and have a drink with Hemingway. They'd want Papa to be their carousing companion, out with them for a night on the town. However, Professor Maine continued, given Hemingway's personality and his characteristics, they wouldn't enjoy the experience all that much. He was short-tempered, prone to insults and cruel jabs if you did not go along with what he said. Professor Maine was trying to get us, a mixed group of graduate and undergraduate students, away from the prepackaged conception of Hemingway as some kind of literary equivalent to the Dos Equis "Most Interesting Man in the World" advertising character. He wanted to remove that illusion, bust that myth if you will, so that we could spend our time thinking about what really mattered with Hemingway: his writing.

I thought I was immune to this thinking, but the realization sank in. I, too, had this image of Hemingway as the larger-than-life cartoon character, the one who would take you out on a rollicking night on the town and then, soon afterward, go out to hunt for wild animals or catch a great fish. While there were actual reasons why this view of Hemingway was so prevalent into people's minds (the historical and biographical records clearly show that Hemingway's voracious alcohol consumption was a fact), it was a distortion that went beyond what the author was like to create something unreal.

What I came to realize was that puncturing that image did not take away from the majesty and importance of the writing. As I read the ending of *A Farewell to Arms*, the Hemingway novel assigned for that course, there was no change in my reaction from the previous times I'd read that novel. The profound pain and despair of Frederic Henry as he loses both his beloved Catherine and their child, describing how "it was like saying good-by to a statue" and "walked back to the hotel in the rain" (Hemingway 1995, 332), were crushing. I was sitting at the front desk of our writing center at Wake Forest. After I read those pages, I had to step away for a moment as that pain overwhelmed me, and I needed a moment alone to compose myself and be ready to greet students looking for help with their assignments. Having this veil pulled from over my eyes did not diminish what I found so powerful in Hemingway's work. In fact, it made me appreciate it even more.

I return to that moment when it comes to the myths surrounding Hemingway. So much of what comes to mind when we talk about Hemingway is that mythos. It's easier to engage with the tall tale than with the man himself in all his complexity. I've also noticed that the Hemingway myth keeps people from picking up his writing, writing that might go a long way in dispelling some of those reductive notions of who he was. For a writer like Hemingway, who has done so much to change our notions of literature and articulated so well on issues of pain and suffering and grief and trauma and love and loss, it is a true shame that the work gets overlooked because of what the myth has done.

In *Authors Inc.: Literary Celebrity in the Modern United States, 1880–1980*, Loren Glass writes that "no study of authorial celebrity in the modern United States would be complete without a consideration of the career of Ernest Hemingway" (2004, 139). Glass makes a particular note of Hemingway's "worldwide public image as 'Papa,' the indestructible U.S. sportsman and aficionado [who] became a veritable paradigm of masculinity in the American cultural imaginary . . . the public personality that Hemingway developed . . . has been an embarrassment for literary critics" (2004, 139–40). This mythos, particularly as it emerged into a more modern media environment able to greatly amplify and distort, was able to run amok and create a myriad of problems for those looking to perform serious considerations of Hemingway. That Papa caricature of Hemingway, which sold men's magazines and exotic travel and liquor and firearms and on and on, was an albatross hung around the necks of serious literary scholars who wished to engage with Hemingway's literature in a serious way.

All this is frustrating on two counts. The first is that Hemingway, the man himself, was plenty interesting even when stripped of the exaggerated elements. Perhaps his feats and actions were not as grand as the imaginary Papa who is so prominent in people's minds, but he's still one of the most fascinating figures in American history. He was friends with many of the great celebrities of his time—Ingrid Bergman, Ava Gardner, Orson Welles, Marlene Dietrich, Gary Cooper—and did meet with some of the major historical figures too (Franklin Delano Roosevelt, Fidel Castro). One does not need tall tales to make Hemingway's life fascinating to an observer.

Perhaps even more than that, this focus on the image of Hemingway that's been peddled keeps us from appreciating Hemingway for his most important contribution to this world: his writing. Because of those assumptions based on the myth of Hemingway, we say to ourselves, "Oh, I wouldn't really like whatever he had to write." This is where that element of embarrassment Glass describes comes into play. Those who might further the *true* appreciation of Hemingway, who might create scholarship that better analyzes or contextualizes his work, are put off from Hemingway because of this cartoon conception of the author they'd been fed. It would be embarrassing to spend one's time and energy studying an author with this kind of an image, and thus they pass.

This is why, as tempting as it is to say that "these are just silly stories. They don't really matter when it comes to Hemingway's literary reputation," we cannot stop there, since they function as impediments to true and full engagement with Hemingway's oeuvre. Other authors suffer from this as well—I think of someone like Jack Kerouac as one whose reputation as an author has been irrevocably damaged because of the image put forth of him—but the myths surrounding Hemingway have done the most damage and have had the most outsized effect.

These myths are not new, as they've been a part of the Hemingway discourse from its very inception. Biographer Carlos Baker sent a letter to Hemingway near the end of the author's life, articulating why he wanted to write a biography of Hemingway, someone who was notoriously distrustful of biographers and literary critics. As I think about *Mythbusting Hemingway*, Baker's words ring in my ears and push me to do this work.

In his letter, Baker writes, "I would like to destroy the legend, puncture the windbags, clear the air a little, and show your achievement in something like its true dimensions. There has been enough malice and lying and misunderstanding" (quoted in Reynolds, *Final Years*, 1999, 259).

Baker speaks in words that would resonate with Hemingway, "destroy" and "puncture" conveying the action and force in which Hemingway was perennially interested. Obviously more important in that statement is Baker's desire to sideline "the legend" as a way of "show[ing]" Hemingway's "achievement in something like its true dimensions." The project is not about diminishing or denigrating but rather about removing all that is not true because what is true is even more special. The man and his work are enough; there doesn't need to be a legend to obscure the feats achieved by the man himself. The work Baker began with his scholarship continues to this day, so much so that one can imagine a modern biographer of Hemingway saying something almost the same as Baker more than fifty years after the biographer and critic wrote those words.

What this book aims to do is address those myths, which so many assume to be the truth about Hemingway, before we engage with the *real* him. These are the things that have become calcified in our collective imaginations and prevent many of us from have a true engagement with one of the greatest authors writing in the English language. Some of these myths will be debunked and proven to be just that—myth. Others might be proven to be true, examples of those spaces where myth and reality line up. But what is important is to get beyond those myths and distortions so that we can appreciate Hemingway and his stellar work unencumbered.

Thomas Bevilacqua
Tallahassee, Florida
2023

Did Hemingway Have an Affair with His Sister-in-Law?

Robert K. Elder and Mark Cirino

In 1925, Ernest Hemingway met two sisters in Paris.

They were aristocrats from Piggott, Arkansas: Pauline and Virginia "Jinny" Pfeiffer. Hemingway, who was finishing his groundbreaking novel *The Sun Also Rises*, was immediately taken with the sisters. Later, the author told a friend that he was more attracted to Jinny, although he liked Pauline's stylish chipmunk coat.

"I'd like to take [Jinny] out in her sister's coat," he said.

Nevertheless, it was Pauline—a fashion journalist for Paris *Vogue*—with whom he began a romance, an affair that ended his first marriage to Hadley Richardson. Jinny would go on to be a close confidant of the author from 1925 to 1940, until Hemingway's bitter divorce from her sister (prompted by, perhaps predictably, another affair).

But in academic circles, Hemingway's intimate relationship with Jinny has been the source of some reexamination.

"I'm personally convinced that Jinny had an affair with Ernest before he became involved with her sister," says Ruth A. Hawkins, author of *Unbelievable Happiness and Final Sorrow: The Hemingway-Pfeiffer Marriage*.

Jinny had at least one late-night encounter with Gertrude Stein, Alice B. Toklas, and Hemingway in 1926, Hawkins writes in her book. After dinner and wine, Hemingway accompanied Jinny "back to her quarters, a visit suggestive of more than conversation."

In 1927, in a letter to his kid sister Sunny, Hemingway described Jinny as "a swell girl . . . she is 25 and as crazy as you are."

But if any physical intimacy between Hemingway and Jinny stretched into her sister's marriage, Hawkins remains skeptical.

"Jinny always loved Ernest," Hawkins says. "She felt like she could have been Mrs. Ernest Hemingway. But she saw how much her sister was in love with him, the nature of that relationship changed."

But there are other signals that Jinny and Hemingway's intimate bond stretched beyond her sister's wedding day. While putting together the book *Hidden Hemingway*, I found a tiny, faded envelope that reads, "Ernest Hemingway. Please do not read until on board."

Inside, written on the reverse of a calling card from Robert Lincoln Kelly, the clandestine message reads, "Just a little some thing to brighten up the way. With love, Jinny."

The undated note—found among the artifacts from his beloved boat, *Pilar*—was most likely written in the 1930s.

There were other signs of a relationship that went beyond friendship. Notably, the first version of his 1927 short story collection *Men without Women* was dedicated to her ("To Jinny, after a hard winter"), though he changed it before publication. Hemingway also carried at least one silver flask with Jinny's name engraved on the cap as late as 1953.

After Ernest and Pauline married, novelist Dawn Powell described Jinny in her diary as "bitterly envious of her sister's position as wife of a world-recognized writer." A friend of Hemingway, Powell observed that Jinny had an unusual attachment to the author, writing that Jinny felt "a bond between herself and [Hemingway]—I shouldn't be surprised if he occasionally gave her reason to believe this."

Even more interesting is a 1997 interview with Pfeiffer family housekeeper Lily Jordan, who recounted Jinny and Hemingway's quail-hunting expeditions. She never remembered them coming back with any game.

"But I never did cook any quails. I thought about that a lot. Why he didn't bring any quails in," Jordan said. "I don't know, maybe he didn't get any."

Although Jinny was romantically linked to men and women, most of her long-term relationships were with women. This sexual flexibility would have been exciting for Hemingway, who often found himself attracted to lesbians. He even accused Jinny of trying to recruit Pauline "into the business" of lesbianism.

Later in life, Jinny's partner Laura Archera became the second wife of author and LSD pioneer Aldous Huxley (*Brave New World*), and they lived together in the Hollywood Hills along with Jinny's two adopted children. Very few letters survive between Hemingway and Jinny, mostly because "an entire correspondence" between them was lost in 1961, when fire destroyed Huxley's home.

However Jinny and Ernest's relationship began, it ended with acrimony. Hemingway blamed Jinny's rumormongering for splitting up his marriage to her sister.

"Virginia's version of my life and conduct is a very fantastic one," he wrote to Pauline and Jinny's mother in 1939. "But she spread it sufficiently and at the right time to break up my home."

Jinny, of course, wasn't spreading rumors. She was correct in her assessment that Hemingway was having an affair with Martha Gellhorn, who would become his third wife. Jinny was fiercely protective of her sister and never forgave Hemingway.

"My aunt . . . hated my father's guts," Hemingway's son Gregory wrote in his 1976 book *Papa: A Personal Memoir*.

Whatever the nature of their relationship was, much mystery remains.

"They had an intimate friendship that went beyond a normal friendship," says Hemingway scholar Hawkins. "I really think that she loved him too."

Verdict: Possible.

Did Hemingway's Suicide Inspire a Famous Spider-Man Story?

Robert K. Elder

When I published the book *Hemingway in Comics* in 2016, I reached out to my favorite writers to ask for cover blurbs; among those writers was J. M. DeMatteis (author of *Moonshadow*, a memorable run on *The Amazing Spider-Man*, and many more titles). I'd spent years documenting Ernest Hemingway's 120-plus appearances in comics alongside Wolverine, Mickey Mouse, and Superman—and exploring the Nobel winner's cultural impact. DeMatteis responded almost immediately and wrote me the most flattering endorsement.

Almost as an afterthought, DeMatteis told me, "Kraven's suicide at the end of *Kraven's Last Hunt* was partially inspired by Hemingway's death. I remember being a kid and hearing about how Hemingway died and that image of the 'Great White Hunter' shoving a rifle in his mouth haunted me for years."

For those who aren't familiar with the story, *Kraven's Last Hunt*— written in 1987 by DeMatteis and illustrated by Mike Zeck—follows Spider-Man villain Kraven the Hunter (a.k.a. Sergei Nikolaevich Kravinoff) into a spiral of mental illness and obsession. But it's not enough for Kraven to simply defeat Spider-Man, whom he's turned into a symbol for everything wrong in his life. To get revenge, Kraven must also become his nemesis and literally assume the mantle of Spider-Man (costume and all) after burying the real webslinger alive. Having accomplished his goals and defeating Vermin, another Spider-Man adversary, Kraven kills himself—an ending that shocked the comic book world.

DeMatteis told me that his first exposure to Hemingway wasn't his short stories or his novels—it was the news of his suicide.

"I knew the name because he was just such a mythic figure—you didn't have to read his books to know who Hemingway was: the macho guy, the hunter, the whole thing," DeMatteis said. "And I remember my friend explaining to me that this guy stuck a rifle in his mouth and blew his head off. And it's shocking at any point. But when you're a kid, and you hear something like that, it's absolutely haunting . . . and it always stayed with me."

While some of the details might not be correct, such as the exact weapon (a rifle vs. a shotgun) and other details (see page 164), the story stayed with DeMatteis.

"It must have just trickled into my unconscious mind and just marinated there all those years. When I was working on Kraven, it just seemed like a natural ending. I don't even know if it was completely conscious," DeMatteis says.

He continues: "It's horrifying. And yet, it's fascinating. It's like the traffic accident that you can't look away from. Suicide in general is always baffling. And to a kid, it's even more baffling. And then it's so graphic, and it's so grotesque. And yet it's the same thing that draws us to horror movies and our fascination with the dark aspects of life. We get fascinated because we want to understand it and absorb it so that we can make sense of the world."

Today, when DeMatteis attends conventions, fans will want to talk to him about *Kraven's Last Hunt*.

"When I go to conventions, I feel like a third of what I sign is probably *Kraven's Last Hunt*. But a third of what I sign is on the exact opposite side of the spectrum, the *Justice League* stories I cowrote with Keith Giffen," says DeMatteis. "What amazes me when I look back is that I was writing those things simultaneously. I was writing this incredibly dark Spider-Man story and these very funny superhero comics at the same time."

Kraven's Last Hunt was so popular that it spawned two sequels, *Amazing Spider-Man: Soul of the Hunter* in 1992 and *Spider-Man:*

The Lost Hunt in 2022–2023. Kraven has had a long history in the Spider-Man universe, debuting in 1964 with *The Amazing Spider-Man* #15. In 2023, the character got his own standalone movie, *Kraven the Hunter*, starring Aaron Taylor-Johnson.

Although the character has continued in different forms, Kraven's suicide was unique in comics—a taboo seldom explored in 1987.

"People can do things that just seem so inexplicable. And I think that's why those things stay with us," DeMatteis says. "And yet, that imagery stayed with me for years. Maybe Hemingway's suicide became a symbol of that dark, incomprehensible part of living—things that, no matter how much we try to explore or explain, will always have a level of mystery to them. But I do not in any way see Hemingway's suicide, or Kraven's, as a noble death."

Verdict: True.

Did a Hemingway Novel Inspire a Country Music Hit Written by the Bee Gees?

Robert K. Elder

The Bee Gees wrote not one but two songs that share the titles of Hemingway novels. The last was the single "For Whom the Bell Tolls" off their 1993 album *Size Isn't Everything*. But their more famous hit was 1983's "Islands in the Stream," originally written for Diana Ross but recorded by Kenny Rogers and Dolly Parton. It became a massive hit, topping the Billboard Hot 100 chart and selling more than two million copies. The Bee Gees would record their own versions of the song in 1998 and 2001.

Islands in the Stream, the novel, was released in 1970 after Hemingway's death. Attempts to reach Barry Gibb, the last surviving member of the Bee Gees, at his home in Florida were unsuccessful. Although multiple articles state that "Islands in the Stream" was inspired by the novel, the Gibb brothers seem to have not talked about it in interviews. But the writing of two songs with Hemingway-related titles seems unlikely to be a coincidence—at least one of the Bee Gees must have been a Hemingway fan.

Verdict: (Likely) True.

Side note: The Bee Gees weren't the only artists to use the title "For Whom the Bell Tolls." It's also the name of a Hemingway-inspired song recorded by the heavy metal band Metallica for their second album, *Ride the Lightning* (1984).

It's also worth noting that Hemingway took his title *For Whom the Bell Tolls* from the English poet and Anglican priest John Donne (1572–1631). The title comes from Donne's 1624 work *Devotions upon Emergent Occasions* and his seventeenth poetic meditation:

> For Whom the Bell Tolls
> by John Donne
> No man is an island,
> Entire of itself.
> Each is a piece of the continent,
> A part of the main.
> If a clod be washed away by the sea,
> Europe is the less.
> As well as if a promontory were.
> As well as if a manor of thine own
> Or of thine friend's were.
> Each man's death diminishes me,
> For I am involved in mankind.
> Therefore, send not to know
> For whom the bell tolls,
> It tolls for thee.

Did Hemingway Box with Heavyweight Champion Gene Tunney?

Thomas Bevilacqua

Hemingway's love of sport, particularly any sport that was violent or exotic, fits in with the image we have of him as a hard-living masculine icon. Fishing, hunting, bullfighting, and boxing were all passions Hemingway possessed that appeared in his fiction. One only needs to think of the bullfighter Pedro Romero in *The Sun Also Rises*, Nick Adams's encounter with Ad Francis in "The Battler," or Jack Brennan's story in "Fifty Grand" to grasp how the world of sport appeared in Hemingway's writing.

But Hemingway did not limit his exploration of these realms to his literary work, as he sought to push his limits by trying them himself. While we know that much of Hemingway's leisure time was spent hunting or fishing, the author also spent some time in the ring, sparring as a boxer. As Hemingway became a writer of greater renown, he began to attract more notable opponents for his forays into the world of boxing. While Hemingway made time to spar, both verbally and physically, with his literary peers, the author also sought opportunities to get into the boxing ring with actual boxers.

Enter Gene Tunney. Tunney held both the American light-heavyweight and heavyweight titles during his career, securing the heavyweight title in 1926 with a victory over Jack Dempsey and then retaining the title with wins over Dempsey and Tom Henney before retiring from the sport in 1928, the same year he was named *The Ring* magazine's "Fighter of the Year."

Tunney was one of the great fighters of the early twentieth century, one who differentiated himself from the competition by being a more cerebral and technical fighter rather than purely a slugger. In a 1961 *Sports Illustrated* piece titled "Double Image of a Champion," Tunney is described as "a stand-up fighter, crafty and graceful, with an accurate, cutting jab and one of the most damaging right-hand punches to the body that boxing has known." That same *Sports Illustrated* article also highlights another way in which Tunney was different from some of his contemporaries, as he mentions that he knew and sometimes fought with a legendary author. "Whenever I went to Cuba, where Ernesto lived, I'd call him and go out to his home," Tunney said. Their interactions make their way into the biographies of Hemingway, as Carlos Baker recounts when the author "knocked off for lunch with Gene Tunney and his wife, went to the cockfights" and then "stood around drinking until the middle of the evening" (1969, 489). In that *Sports Illustrated* piece, Tunney also notes another activity the two would engage in: "We'd spar sometimes. Barehanded, no gloves."

In his book *Shadow Box*, the writer George Plimpton confirmed these sessions did in fact happen, providing greater insight into something that happened at one of these sparring matches that had an outsize impact. Plimpton recalls "often hear[ing] a rumor that Hemingway had sparred with Tunney" and then "check[ing] it out with Tunney's son" (2016, 60) who confirmed the incident occurred. "[A]t the *finca*," Plimpton writes, after talking with Tunney's son, "the two began shuffling around the big living room and Hemingway . . . threw a low punch, perhaps out of clumsiness, but it hurt [and] outraged Tunney" (60–61). After this, Tunney made it clear that, given the fact he was a professional fighter and a former heavyweight champion, he could do real damage to Hemingway if fought in this way, forcefully telling Hemingway, "*Don't you ever do that again!*" As a result, Hemingway never asked the fighter to step back into the ring again (2016, 61).

A similar account appears in the memoir of Finca Vigía majordomo René Villarreal. He remembers when "Gene Tunney, the former heavyweight champion . . . came for lunch one day. . . . Papa and Tunney drank heavily that afternoon, and it wasn't long before they were exchanging light punches in the dining room. It all seemed harmless enough until one of them let go and punched a bit too hard. Then it quickly escalated into a grudge match" (2009, 119).

In addition to these living-room sparring sessions at the Finca Vigía, there was another bout between the two that Mary Dearborn identifies in her biography of the author. After visiting his fourth wife's parents in New Orleans for Thanksgiving 1947, Hemingway and Mary traveled to New York where "Ernest finally[1] got Gene Tunney to spar with him, probably at George Brown's gym on West 47th Street" (2017, 496) where a similar scene transpired—namely, Hemingway getting a little too overzealous and Tunney, though this time with a "good little liver punch" rather than his words, making it clear he did not want to proceed (2017, 497). While Hemingway and Tunney might have gotten into the ring more than once, the "main event" between the two, the one that had the lasting impact on Hemingway, was their bout in Finca Vigía's living room that Plimpton recounts.

It made sense that Hemingway would seek out a heavyweight champion for some sparring experience. It also made sense that Tunney would keep the company of a writer like Hemingway. In a way that was different from fighters who came before or since, Tunney displayed an interest in literature. Jack Cavanaugh recounts this in his biography of Tunney, writing of one time when the fighter "was scheduled to go on a walking tour in France and Germany with Thornton Wilder. . . . Before his return, Tunney would also meet a number of other noted writers, such as George Bernard Shaw, H. G. Wells, Ernest Hemingway, Arnold Bennett, and F. Scott Fitzgerald," with "Tunney . . . pleasantly surprised to find out that most of the literary lions he met on his trip had an interest in boxing" (2006, 385). Tunney even entered into Hemingway's arena by writing a book titled *A Man Must Fight*, which was published in 1932 and allowed the fighter to both reflect on his boxing career and offer his thoughts on the sport.

Tunney was not the only famous boxer with whom Hemingway engaged. As Baker notes, in 1935, Hemingway also "sparred a few 'exhibition' rounds with Tom Heeney" (1969, 274). Then there was the fighter with whom Hemingway "sparred" outside of the ring. Jack Dempsey, whom Tunney beat twice to claim the heavyweight title, knew the author. Roger Kahn, in his biography of Dempsey, recounts the fighter saying, "There were a lot of Americans in Paris and I sparred with a couple, just to be obliging. . . . But there was one fellow I wouldn't mix with. That was Ernest Hemingway" (2000, 271). Dempsey "had this sense that Hemingway, who really thought he could box, would come out of the corner like a madman" and "to stop him, [Dempsey] would have to hurt him badly. . . . That's why [he] never sparred with him" (2000, 271), echoing Hemingway's failed sparring session with Tunney, his unwillingness to consider who he was sparring against and what damage that opponent could do if pushed to the brink. Dempsey had also engaged "in a 'playful' sparring match" with Al Jolson that had resulted in the singer and actor being hurt, which gave Dempsey more motivation not to trade a few blows with Hemingway (Dearborn 2017, 436). Kahn speculates that an antipathy between Hemingway and Dempsey came about because "Dempsey dismiss[ed] boxing Hemingway with an easy putdown, and Hemingway persisting and Dempsey . . . now annoyed, sneering or perhaps even laughing in Hemingway's face" (2000, 291). As Dempsey put it, "I never ducked a fighter, just a writer" (2000, 271).

Verdict: True.

Did Hemingway Meet J. D. Salinger?

Thomas Bevilacqua

Hemingway could be fiercely competitive with fellow writers, at times treating them like enemy combatants rather than peers and collaborators in the work of literature. His relationships with F. Scott Fitzgerald, Sherwood Anderson, and Gertrude Stein all reflected a certain competitiveness, and they frayed due in part to Hemingway's combative nature. Hemingway was dismissive of James Jones and his novel *From Here to Eternity*, which he said "is much too long and much too bitching and his one fight . . . is almost musical comedy" (*Selected Letters*, 2003, 721), perhaps owing to Jones' position as a fellow author at Scribner's and thus getting attention from Hemingway's publisher. All this to say that Hemingway could be unpleasant when it came to interactions with those who also participated in the literary life.

However, Hemingway offered support and guidance to one author whom he met while in Europe at the end of World War II. During that period, with France being liberated in the wake of D-Day, Hemingway encountered J. D. Salinger, who was then serving in the US Army and years away from writing his famed novel *The Catcher in the Rye*.

The first meeting between these two writers occurred in Paris shortly after its liberation at the hands of the Allied Forces. "Hemingway was serving as a war correspondent for *Collier's* and had reportedly managed to slip into Paris ahead of the liberating armies," Kenneth Slawenski notes in his biography of Salinger (2012, 100). As Salinger's regiment made its way to the French capital following the battle at Normandy, Salinger knew he could find Hemingway at the Hotel Ritz's bar. Terry Mort describes how "Hemingway was enjoying his time at the Ritz, not only with Mary but also with a group of well-wishers and old acquaintances" (2016, 211) amid the recently liberated Paris. "Hemingway greeted Salinger like an old friend" when the young man came into the bar and he "claimed to be familiar with Salinger's writings" (Slawenski 2012, 100). After "Hemingway asked if Salinger had any new works on him," the young author "locate[d] a copy of *The Saturday Evening Post* containing 'Last Day of the Last Furlough,'" which "Hemingway read . . . and was impressed" (101). Baker describes how Salinger "found Hemingway both friendly and generous, not at all impressed by his own eminence, and 'soft'—as opposed to the hardness and toughness which some of his writing suggested" (1969, 420). For Salinger, a burgeoning young writer, this meeting with Hemingway left him, as Baker describes it, "in a state of mild exaltation" (420).

But that would not be the only meeting between the two monumental figures in American literature. "[T]hey meet again," Brewster Chamberlin writes, "during a lull in the Hürtgenwald fighting . . . drink[ing] champagne in [Hemingway's] cabin" (2015, 251). Dearborn goes into more detail, describing how "Salinger . . . found Ernest in the PR office" in Hürtgenwald, "reclining on a couch, wearing a sun visor, writing on a yellow pad" (2017, 472). Hemingway "was glad to see Salinger . . . and he broke out a bottle of champagne" (472).

But even though "the common understanding is that Hemingway and Salinger met only [those] two times, in Paris and in the Hürtgen Forest . . . another meeting took place during the Battle of the Bulge" (Salerno and Shields 2014, 152–53). As Charles Meyers, a fellow member of the Counter Intelligence Corps with Salinger, recalled, "Hemingway was at that time attached to the 4th [Fourth Infantry Division, which included Salinger]" and that "Jerry gave him some of his stories to read" (quoted in Salerno and Shields 2014, 153). After giving his stories to Hemingway, Salinger "showed . . . a note penciled on a piece of brown paper bag which Hemingway had sent him . . . commend[ing] Jerry's 'ear' and prais[ing] the considerable talent and promise of his stories" (quoted in Salerno and Shields 2014, 153).

Though they would not meet in person again, Salinger did continue his correspondence with Hemingway following World War II's conclusion. In Brewster Chamberlin's *The Hemingway Log*, he notes that on July 27, Salinger wrote Hemingway a letter saying that "on the day the Germans surrendered (May 8) he fell into a serious depression and contemplated shooting himself in the palm of his hand with his GI issue .45 caliber automatic pistol, whereupon he knew he needed help and checked himself into the hospital" (2015, 258) though "It wasn't one event that put Salinger in the hospital. . . . It was a culmination of events: going through eleven months of war, being forced to witness atrocities beyond human imagination" (Salerno and Shields 2014, 169). Salinger's letter to Hemingway reflected a connection between the two, bridging both the men and their fiction. Salinger scholar Eberhard Alsen describes how Salinger "wrote Hemingway about his breakdown because he knew Hemingway had seen combat firsthand. . . . Salinger probably felt Hemingway would understand what he was going through" (quoted in Salerno and Shields 2014, 170). Though Salinger did not experience the physical wounding that Hemingway did while at the Italian front in World War I, Salinger experienced similar psychological trauma that would affect him and his view of the world for the rest of his life. Lawrence Grobel said, "I don't have any doubt it [Salinger's breakdown] had an enormous effect on his sense of humanity. Why do people go to war? Why do they kill each other? How can there be a Dachau or an Auschwitz? He had seen the other side of man" (quoted in Salerno and Shields 2014, 169). Through their experiences with war, both Hemingway and Salinger confronted the ugliness and destructive nature of men in this world and subsequently wrestled with those notions in their writing.

Those meetings with Hemingway sustained Salinger emotionally beyond the end of the war and into the literary career that would yield such great impact on American letters. "Salinger derived great personal strength through his relationship with Ernest Hemingway," Slawenski notes in his biography. "[He was] grateful for Hemingway's friendship and thanked him for providing rare moments of hope" (2012, 101–2). Salinger found a way to acknowledge and pay homage to Hemingway in print. In *The Catcher in the Rye*, Holden Caufield recounts how his brother had him read Hemingway's *A Farewell to Arms*. Holden, unsurprisingly, tossed off Hemingway's book as being phony, though perhaps being dismissed by Holden as phony is a real compliment.

Slawenski notes how "Salinger perceived his time with Hemingway as a generational passing of the torch . . . he went to the Hotel Ritz not to pay homage but to collect what he considered to be his rightful inheritance" (2012, 101), but the moment served as both a reverential event and one that highlighted the passage of time. In it, two writers who would go on to define American literature crossed paths and spent time together, the young up-and-comer venerating the old lion. While the torch would not completely be passed, as Hemingway had yet to write *The Old Man and the Sea* (which would win him numerous awards and secure the Nobel Prize in Literature), this was a moment where the previous and the rising generations of authors came into contact. It seems like something that would be too scripted, too good to be true. And yet it was.

Verdict: True.

Were Mojitos Hemingway's Favorite Drink?

Thomas Bevilacqua

The voracious consumption of alcohol is a major component of Hemingway's mythos. One will find drinks on menus around the world that, allegedly, Hemingway invented or are named in his honor. You can walk into a bar just about anywhere and order a Death in the Afternoon or an Islands in the Stream, and you will not (necessarily) be given a book written by Hemingway in return. There are more bars around the world with stories about how Hemingway once drank there than perhaps about any other figure in modern memory. There is even a brand of rum that bears the same name as Hemingway's beloved boat, *Pilar*.

One of those bars with which Hemingway is associated is La Bodeguita del Medio in Havana, Cuba. At that bar, one can find a napkin featuring the following (allegedly) written in Hemingway's handwriting: "My Mojito in La Bodeguita My Daiquiri in El Floridita." Each bar was known for making those respective cocktails, as it was either invented or perfected there. La Bodeguita del Medio is regarded as the birthplace of the mojito, or at least the place where the drink entered the upper stratosphere of cocktail consumption, while El Floridita was well-known for its daiquiris. Because of that note found at La Bodeguita, the notion of Hemingway as a regular mojito drinker—drinking them at the same clip as the daiquiris that would come to bear his name—was born. While there is clear evidence that Hemingway partook of the daiquiris from El Floridita, the association with the mojito is much less clearly determined and appears to be a flight of fancy rather than anything based in fact.

For one thing, the authenticity of the note hanging on display in La Bodeguita has been called into question. Cocktail writer and historian Wayne Curtis goes so far as to recount how "some have suggested that Hemingway wasn't a regular patron [at La Bodeguita] as he was at El Floridita, but that he stretched this out one night when in his cups at the behest of a persistent, marketing-minded bar manager" to offer up this written endorsement (2018, 238). That note was one likely composed under duress or at least aided by numerous drinks. Brewster Chamberlin takes things as step further: "I have carefully examined the handwritten note attributed to Hemingway and I am convinced that he did not in fact write it. The handwriting is not his" (quoted in Greene 2012, 171). For the author of *The Hemingway Log*—one who pored over Hemingway's handwritten letters, notebooks, fishing logs, and manuscripts, someone who certainly possessed a familiarity with the author's handwriting—to make that claim stands as a convincing piece of evidence that the piece of writing that was displayed in La Bodeguita was not written by the hand of Ernest Hemingway.

Beyond this analysis, there is another reason to doubt that when Hemingway had a drink, he most frequently reached for a mojito, a reason based on what we know about Hemingway and his tastes. Hemingway's preference for his unique daiquiri from El Floridita came about for a very specific reason. Wayne Curtis describes the day Constantino Ribalaigua Vert, the owner and proprietor of El Floridita, saw "a scruffy, bearish man" in his establishment who "saw the daiquiris lined up on the bar [and] his curiosity was piqued" (2018, 171). Because he was a diabetic, Hemingway tried to stay away from especially sugary cocktails. The mixture that became known as Hemingway's daiquiri came about for just that reason. Hemingway tried the daiquiri at El Floridita, giving his blessing but saying next time he would prefer less of the sugar and double the alcohol. In Curtis's book *And a Bottle of Rum: A History of the New World in*

Ten Cocktails, he includes the recipes for famous rum-based cocktails. Included in there is Hemingway's daiquiri, from which, he is careful to note, "Hemingway omitted the simple syrup" (2018, 277).

What is most revealing about this anecdote, for the purposes of discerning whether Hemingway did in fact drink mojitos, is his desire to avoid sugary drinks. The mojito is a cocktail in which the sugar plays a significant role, using at least one ounce of simple syrup. That is not to say that sweeter cocktails did not appear on Hemingway's radar. As Philip Greene notes, "The Jack Rose comes to mind" when it comes to cocktails associated with Hemingway that are on the sweeter side, "but that was from 1926's *The Sun Also Rises* [when] Hemingway was twenty-seven, not yet worried about sugar" (2012, 170). When Hemingway made his way to Cuba, he was much older, and his concern with his sugar intake (and how it would react with his diabetes) was much more pressing.

Hemingway's desire to eschew sweeter drinks might have come about for yet another reason. In his cocktail guide and history of tropical drinks titled *Potions of the Caribbean*, Jeff "Beachbum" Berry writes of how "Hemingway . . . was an alcoholic. And alcoholics do not make good drinks. They make strong drinks. They're not interested in striking the right balance of sweet, sour, strong, and weak" (2013, 142). Thus a drink like the mojito, not an especially strong drink, would not be to Hemingway's liking. The other component to Hemingway's variation on the daiquiri, double the rum in addition to losing the sugar, reflects this. In fact, when one sees a "Hemingway Daiquiri" on the cocktail menu at various bars, it will be identified as a modified version or that establishment's version of the cocktail as though anyone who was not actually Hemingway would want to drink that drink according to Papa's measurements.

Hemingway's love for the daiquiri, particularly the way it was made at El Floridita, made its way into his writing. In the posthumously published *Islands in the Stream*, Hemingway describes his protagonist, Thomas Hudson, who "had been ashore about four days [in Cuba] when he got really drunk. . . . He had drunk double frozen

29

daiquiris, the great ones that Constante made, that had no taste of alcohol and felt, as you drank them, the way downhill glacier skiing feels running through powder snow and, after the sixth and eighth, felt like downhill glacier skiing feels when you are running unroped" (1970, 211).

Hemingway refers to both the drink, the bar that made them, and the bartender who popularized them in *Islands in the Stream*. But the mojito, this drink that has somehow come to be seen as a Hemingway staple alongside the daiquiri, does not appear in a similar light anywhere in Hemingway's writing. Philip Greene notes how "with nearly every other drink . . . I can place the particular drink either into Hemingway's hands, from biographies, memoirs, or letters, or into his characters' hands, from his prose" and yet "[n]ot so with the Mojito" as he has "not yet encountered a single reference to either the drink or the Bodeguita" (2012, 169). In the volume of Michael Reynolds's Hemingway biography focusing on the time in his life when he would have been in Cuba, we find many references to El Floridita (indexed with many other bars that were important to Hemingway) yet no reference to La Bodeguita.

It is likely that Hemingway drank mojitos, perhaps even many of them. As Matthew J. Bruccoli notes, "It is a safe generalization that Hemingway tried every cocktail ever mixed" (quoted in Felten 2007). Curtis also, quite correctly, notes that the writer "was not especially picky when it came to alcohol" (2018, 173), and thus one can certainly imagine Hemingway having one (if not more) mojitos in his life. But that it would become the drink with which Hemingway was most closely associated, the drink ascribed to him in *Hemingway & Bailey's Bartending Guide to Great American Writers*, is a bit of a stretch.

Verdict: False.

Was Hemingway Investigated
by the FBI?

Thomas Bevilacqua

Toward the end of his life, Ernest Hemingway was prone to flights of paranoia and extreme worry. These worries, perhaps exacerbated by the repeated head trauma he'd suffered throughout his life, might have been about his health or his financial well-being or the status of friends and family members. Sometimes those concerns could reach beyond and into something much bigger: full-blown paranoia. Hemingway believed that he was the subject of an investigation into his life and affairs by the US government and that his native government saw him as a potential threat. The Federal Bureau of Investigation was the agency Hemingway suspected of prying into his affairs. However, while it might seem a bit fanciful to think that the US intelligence apparatus at the height of the Cold War would focus their attention on an aging author, recent disclosures seem to corroborate Hemingway's concerns and give us evidence that he was (technically) under investigation by the FBI.

The FBI's interest in Hemingway dated back to 1937 and "his rabble rousing speech at the American Writers Congress" (Dearborn 2017, 429), while a mutual antipathy emerged between the bureau and Hemingway, as the writer "heard it said that many FBI agents were Catholics and that the bureau was a known friend to the Church, concluding that FBI agents were automatic Franco sympathizers" (Dearborn 2017, 430). Owing to this, Hemingway would fit the profile of someone whom the bureau would designate a person worthy of investigation. The bureau's file on Hemingway included a memo that stated, "It is known that Hemingway and his assistant, Gustavo Durán, have a . . . personal hostility to the FBI on an ideological basis, especially Hemingway, as he considers the FBI anti-Liberal, pro-Fascist and dangerous as developing into an American Gestapo" (quoted in Reynolds, *Final Years*, 1999, 75).

The FBI was also inclined to keep a watchful eye on Hemingway for the "work" he did to help their cause, as he provided information to the American embassy in Havana while living there. With the blessing of Spruille Braden, who was the United States ambassador to Cuba from 1942 to 1945, Hemingway established what he referred to as the "Crook Factory." The "Crook Factory" was a form of counter-intelligence focused on keeping tabs on those who were sympathetic to Francisco Franco, the fascist dictator who ruled Spain following his victory in the Spanish Civil War, and who aligned themselves with the fascist cause. However, while this group might have had grand ideas about the importance of the work they did, in reality "the meetings turned into drinking parties" and "they never succeeded in developing any information of much value, and the local FBI agent dismissed the whole idea" (Mort 2016, 31). This level of awareness would reflect Andrew Farah's assertion that "the information in the file as it existed was certainly not news to him," as "he could have guessed its contents on the basis of his own experience and contacts with the FBI men" (2017, 68).

Meyers notes that "the file was extremely repetitive, and became unintentionally funny when the solemn bureaucrats reported the bizarre behavior of the author" (1985, 367), which reflects a sense in which those running this investigation did not take the matter as one of great concern. Andrew Farah notes that "a recurrent theme in Hemingway's late-life paranoia was the FBI and its continual 'surveillance'" (2017, 64). Farah also points out that "the mere fact that [Hemingway] had a file was not unusual for a celebrity of his era, particularly given his connections during the Spanish Civil War" and "thus, the existence of a file does not negate his paranoia. His delusions were independent of its existence, and he was not under surveillance" (2017, 65). The fact that there had been some investigation was not particularly noteworthy and was taken "no more seriously than any of the other suspected Communists in America during that period, especially those who had supported the Loyalist cause in the Spanish Civil War" (Hutchisson 2016, 243–44).

Nevertheless, the surveillance of Hemingway performed by the FBI and his awareness of it potentially had serious consequences. Many have contended that the presence of the FBI spying on him drove Hemingway to take his own life. A. E. Hotchner, friend and biographer of the author, stated this with the greatest conviction. In a 2011 *New York Times* piece, he describes how "in the years since [Hemingway's suicide], I have tried to reconcile Ernest's fear of the F.B.I., which I regretfully misjudged, with the reality of the F.B.I. file. I now believe he truly sensed the surveillance, and that it substantially contributed to his anguish and his suicide" (Hotchner 2011). Nicholas Reynolds notes that "Hotchner understood Hemingway's state of mind better than he understood the Bureau's intent" (2017, 263). For while the bureau was interested in Hemingway's actions and affairs, there was not a full-blown investigation and especially not one that was up to the standards that Hemingway imagined through his paranoia. But as Reynolds writes about Hotchner's understanding of Hemingway and his experience during that period, it might not have felt that way to the author, as he "was unravelling, like a length of coarse rope frayed at both ends" (Hutchisson 2016, 244). Though the FBI's intent might not have been a full-blown special investigation of Hemingway, just the specter of a routine one in Hemingway's mind (which was dealing with a great deal at that point) was perhaps enough to aggravate his already fragile mental state.

Verdict: (Technically) True.

Did Hemingway Shoot a Toilet?

Thomas Bevilacqua

Among the many things Hemingway possessed were powerful feelings and emotions, which became even more prominent as the author aged. While Hemingway was famous for his image of the iceberg that he used to describe his approach to fiction, in his own life, the most appropriate image might be a volcano poised to erupt with the slightest prompting. These strong emotions tended to show themselves in Hemingway's romantic life, which is perhaps not surprising for a man who was married four times and rumored to have had affairs with famous and glamorous women. Michael Reynolds describes the "manic ardor" Hemingway possessed that "overwhelmed" his (eventual) fourth wife Mary Welsh (*Final Years*, 1999, 114). These powerful feelings manifested in eruptions of emotions and violent action. Those emotions manifested when Hemingway, in a rage, shot and destroyed a hotel-room toilet.

Mary's husband at the time, Noel Monks, was making her ability to obtain a divorce exceedingly difficult. "Mary wrote to Noel that she would now take the necessary first steps for a divorce," but Noel responded by being "more vindictive than she had expected . . . order[ing] the Time office to sell her things[,] and then [he] withdrew all the money in their joint bank account" (Kert 1998, 416). Noel's ability to impede Mary from moving on and starting her new life with Hemingway enraged him, which culminated in the author firing the toilet-bowl-destroying shot. Hemingway "placed a photograph of [Mary's] Australian husband in the toilet bowl [and] blasted it with a machine pistol and flooded their room at the Ritz" (Meyers

1985, 416) in Paris. Mary Dearborn corroborates this and provides greater detail into why exactly this happened. She recounts how initially Hemingway "placed [the picture] in the fireplace and took aim at it," but "Buck [Lanham] yanked Ernest's arm up, aborting what might have been, because of ricochets, a very dangerous thought" (2017, 467). Hemingway "fired at [the picture] six times," destroying the toilet bowl "at a time when porcelain was virtually unobtainable" (467).

Timothy Christian describes how the incident was, to some degree, incited by Charles T. "Buck" Lanham, the commander of the Twenty-Second Infantry Regiment, who had become friendly with the author as he observed and wrote about the actions of the American military during its move through and liberation of Axis-occupied Europe. Hemingway's essay "War in the Siegfried Line" depicts Lanham and his exploits, particularly at breaking through the line Hemingway mentioned in his title. Christian writes that "Buck presented Ernest with an elegant wooden, velvet-lined case containing two German machine pistols, complete with ammunition" that "Ernest wanted to try" (2022, 99). After he "seized a photograph of Noel and Mary from the mantelpiece," he took aim at the man "he called . . . an idiot for his letters to Mary" and "fired at Noel's mouth, creating a gaping hole" (Christian 2022, 99). Perhaps most important when it comes to determining the validity of this story, Mary Welsh Hemingway corroborates the tale of Hemingway's pistol-aided destruction of a toilet in her autobiography *How It Was*, clarifying that it was "a pleasant photograph of Noel Monks and [herself]" (1976, 147).

Verdict: True.

Were Hemingway's Early Manuscripts Lost?

Thomas Bevilacqua

Just as he was beginning his literary career, Ernest Hemingway experienced a setback that might have derailed other writers, keeping them from achieving whatever literary aspirations they had. Instead, an event became an enormous part of Hemingway's mythos, distinguishing him in literary history, and might have pushed him to develop the more modern writing style for which he would become forever associated. That event occurred when Hemingway's early manuscripts, the work he created as he moved to Paris and began his career as a writer, were lost forever.

On December 2, 1922, Hemingway's then wife Hadley planned to travel by train from Paris to Lausanne, Switzerland, to see him as he was covering the Lausanne Peace Conference, which produced the Treaty of Lausanne between the Allied nations in World War I and the Ottoman Empire. Hadley brought with her a suitcase filled with the manuscripts on which Hemingway had been working. Hadley said she packed up Hemingway's work because of "Ernest's letters singing high praises of Lincoln Steffens . . . to whom [Hadley] felt certain Ernest would want to show" his writing (quoted in Diliberto 2011, 129). Jack Hemingway, Ernest's child with Hadley, said that "all I ever heard from both my parents [about the lost manuscripts] was that my father asked her to bring the manuscripts" (quoted in Diliberto 2011, 129). While Hadley made it to Lausanne, that suitcase containing the manuscripts would not, as it was stolen from the Gare de Lyon. Carlos Baker recounts the "frozen horror" (1969,

103) in which Hadley found herself after realizing that those manuscripts had been stolen from the train station, and when she arrived in Lausanne, "[s]he was crying so much that she had trouble explaining what had happened" (Diliberto 2011, 130). Though Hemingway "was tender and patient and seemed less upset than Hadley . . . [s]he, more than anyone, knew what those stolen manuscripts represented [and] . . . the degree of anger and frustration that must be boiling up inside" Hemingway (Kert 1998, 127).

Hemingway writes about this in *A Moveable Feast*, his memoir of those early years in Paris, describing the time "when everything I had written was stolen in Hadley's suitcase . . . at the Gare de Lyon when she was bringing the manuscripts down to me to Lausanne as a surprise . . . the originals, the typescripts and the carbons" (2009, 69). Hemingway goes on to describe how he "hired someone to cover for [him] on [his] newspaper job" and "took the train for Paris" where he found "it was true all right" (2009, 70).

Though the bulk of those stories were lost forever, there were two stories that Hemingway still had. One was "My Old Man," since "Lincoln Steffens had sent it out to some editor who sent it back," while "Up in Michigan" was "in a drawer somewhere" (2009, 69) back in Paris.

Hemingway also writes in *A Moveable Feast*, "I remember what I did in the night after I let myself into the flat and found it was true" (2009, 70). However, what exactly Hemingway did after returning to Paris and discovering that the manuscripts were indeed lost "remained his secret for the rest of his life" (Baker 1969, 103), as no biographer or scholar has been able to determine the answer, speaking to the enormity of their loss to the author (despite his later protestations that the loss of the writing did not matter all that much).

Michael Reynolds recorded that one of the pieces in that lost suitcase was "the Chicago novel, the one set at the war, [which] was not worth the grieving" as it was "untouched for months" while "the lost poems were expendable" (*Paris Years*, 1999, 89) as well. However, what hurt most was the loss of "the stories and . . . the Paris sketches," though it was "great but not total" (*Paris Years*, 1999, 89).

Hemingway's true agitation was apparent in a 1923 letter sent to Ezra Pound. Hemingway tells Pound about "the loss of [his] Juvenilia" (2013, 6). Hemingway assumed that Pound would be in favor of his losing these earlier, rougher works ("You, naturally, would say 'Good' etc."). Hemingway regarded that kind of thinking as nothing more than "that stuff you feed the troops." Still frustrated, Hemingway wrote, "I aint yet reached that mood. I worked 3 years on the damn stuff," mentioning "that Paris 1922 stuff [he] fancied" (2013, 6). Losing the stories was quite a shock to the young and developing Hemingway, despite his claims that "it was probably good . . . to lose early work." Hemingway went on to describe this event in his memoir *A Moveable Feast*, using the same language as in his letter to Pound as he described the notion of being better off for the loss of those manuscripts as "all that stuff you feed the troops" (2009, 70).

What Hemingway wrote in *A Moveable Feast*, decades after the loss of that writing, presents a version of the story that emphasized his resilience in overcoming this calamity. But we see that his actual reaction was, understandably, one of greater frustration and anger. Perhaps it was his own desire to make a myth, that even this great loss that would have wounded a lesser writer was something he was able to overcome. It also lifted some of the blame from Hadley, something that Hemingway might have been seeking to do more broadly in writing that memoir.

That line about "feed[ing] the troops" appeared in Hemingway's fiction as well. In *The Garden of Eden*, after Catherine has burned his clippings or stories, David Bourne's current lover Marita tries to console him, to which he replies, "Don't buck me up . . . I wrote it and I wrote what she burned. Don't give me the stuff they feed the troops" (1986, 230). The way Hemingway draws on this experience of losing his work, though admittedly through different circumstances in *The Garden of Eden*, perhaps displays the latent frustration and anger at losing those manuscripts that remained in his mind throughout his life. Catherine's destruction of those stories is painted as the final straw or last recrimination that ultimately dissolves this fraught relationship. An interesting note from the final volume of Michael Reynolds's exploration of Hemingway's life forges those connections. Reynolds recounts how "Hemingway's memory and his fiction would return again and again to the apartment above the sawmill on rue Notre Dame des Champs where he first found his voice . . . produc[ing] his Paris memoir—*A Moveable Feast*" as well as "out of the same matrix came a different story of a Paris writer, David Bourne in *The Garden of Eden*" (*Final Years*, 1999, 137–38). Perhaps as Hemingway thought back to that time, one punctuated with the loss of those manuscripts, he drew upon it as he wrote his fictional story of an American writer in Paris at around the same time. Hemingway further engaged with that moment in his fiction through "The Strange Country," which was part of an early version of *Islands in the Stream* and is presented as an unpublished short story in the *Complete Short Stories of Ernest Hemingway* collection.

Though he tried to hide his anger at the lost manuscripts, that trauma stayed with Hemingway for the rest of his life. Hemingway "would become visibly tense whenever the subject was mentioned" even "in 1959 when he was celebrating his sixtieth birthday" (Kert 1998, 128). Other biographers identify it as "the first disastrous blow to their [Ernest and Hadley's] marriage" and have seen how "the loss was irrevocably connected in Hemingway's mind with sexual infidelity, and he equated the lost manuscripts with lost love," as "now [he] had something to hold against her—for he never forgot an injury—and would later use it to justify his callous behavior" (Meyers 1985, 70).

While the loss of those stories might have been a frustrating shock to Hemingway, they also pushed him into the deep and led him to adopt the writing style for which he became renowned. In her biography of Hemingway, Verna Kale describes how "the suitcase theft had opened up the opportunity, and that spring Hemingway was finally able to write something new" as "'Out of Season' . . . the first short story Hemingway completed after the suitcase theft, that represents the young author's initial experiment with a 'new theory'" of writing (2016, 42–43). This event did more to burnish a kind of mythical concept of Hemingway divorced from the reality. As Lesley Blume writes, losing those manuscripts and being forced to start over "would instead make [Hemingway] appear as something of an Athena springing fully formed from Zeus's forehead" (2016, 36). The year 1922 produced such major works of modernist literature as James Joyce's *Ulysses*, T. S. Eliot's *The Wasteland*, and Virginia Woolf's *Jacob's Room*. How much better would it make that narrative if Hemingway was pushed into his own modern, unique literary form in that year as well?

For someone like Hemingway, it is appropriate that even the truth could create a myth that could be used to augment and embellish his stature. Hemingway's reality features moments that lift him up to the realm of the mythic, which highlights how he does not need those tall tales and untruths to have a life that towers above the average writer. Marc Seals describes how "Hemingway repeatedly wrote about this one particular traumatic experience" (2009, 76) and thus sees it as "quite possible that Hemingway was writing and rewriting about the loss of his manuscripts in an attempt, perhaps unconscious, at psychological discovery (or recovery) and perhaps even healing" (78). The recurrence of this moment in Hemingway's writing, coupled with the biographical and historical record documenting it, speaks to its veracity as something that did transpire and left a mark on the author for the rest of his life.

Verdict: True.

Did Hemingway Survive Multiple Plane Crashes?

Thomas Bevilacqua

Living one's life as a man of daring and adventure will often lead to countless injuries and brushes with death. That was certainly the case for Hemingway, whose life seemed to be an unending stream of injuries and accidents. The author suffered gunshot wounds from fishing expeditions gone wrong,[2] a car accident in 1944 London that "open[ed] a huge gash in his skull . . . giving him a severe concussion" that "would today be called a traumatic brain injury" that could be defined as "life-changing" (Dearborn 2017, 448), and a head injury caused by putting a skylight down on his head (the perils of using the bathroom late at night) and causing a wound whose bleeding could be stopped only with "30 thicknesses of toilet paper . . . and a tourniquet of kitchen towel and a stick of kindling wood" (*Letters*, 2015, 373). Hemingway was something of a magnet for physical harm. In books on the author, one will find entries in the index identifying the times he was injured (and, quite frequently, injuries that affected his head).

Save for his wounding on the Italian front during World War I, there was no incident as painful as what happened to him in early 1954. Just like that traumatic war wound that would become a part of the great narrative of Hemingway's life, the multiple plane crashes Hemingway endured and survived would further the sense that Hemingway was somehow indestructible. Actually, though, they left him with maladies that might have hastened the end of his life.

In late January 1954, Hemingway and his fourth wife, Mary, were on a safari in Africa that began the year before. While in

Uganda, they planned to photograph Murchison Falls, a waterfall at Lake Alberta, from overhead. As Carlos Baker recounted, the author and his wife "circled the falls three times, winging over for the picture taking," but "somewhere in the third circle a flight of ibis suddenly crossed the path of the plane. As [the pilot] dived to avoid them," the plane "struck an abandoned telegraph wire which stretched across the gorge . . . nick[ing] the propeller and rak[ing] the tail assembly" (1969, 519). Mary, who felt "her heart . . . pounding fast" and "a sharp pain in her left chest," and Ernest, "in obvious pain from the damage to his right arm and shoulder" as he tended to his wife (Christian 2022, 220–21), got the attention of another plane that could take them to receive medical care.

As the second flight prepared to take off, "the right engine caught fire, igniting a ruptured fuel tank, quickly turning the plane into a death trap" (*Final Years*, 1999, 273), as "Mary saw flames outside her window before she could get her seatbelt undone" and she and Roy Marsh, their pilot, were forced to get out of the plane through a broken window while Ernest forced his way out of a jammed door (Christian 2022, 222). While the first crash served as, relatively speaking, an inconvenience, "the second crash was much worse than the first and seriously injured Hemingway" (Meyers 1985, 505). After barely escaping the flaming plane, Hemingway was left grievously wounded: "Behind his left ear, the scalp was torn and clear fluid was leaking . . . one of his kidneys was badly hurt, his overworked liver damaged, his shoulder dislocated, his lower intestine collapsed and he suffered temporary loss of hearing in his left ear and vision in his left eye" (*Final Years*, 1999, 274). The crash was, in Reynolds's estimation, Hemingway's fourth concussion in ten years, and "celebrating their double escape at the bar" with drinks "was guaranteed to make the concussion worse" (*Final Years*, 1999, 274). Jeffrey Meyers uncovers further maladies suffered from this second crash, including "his sphincter muscle [being] paralyzed by compressed vertebrae on the iliac nerve [and] suffer[ing] from internal bleeding, nausea, and retching" (1985, 505). For the then fifty-four-year-old author, with all the hard living he'd done up to that point, these were extremely serious and painful injuries.

Given the severity of these plane crashes, particularly that second one, many in the international press corps started reporting that the author had died as a result. As he recuperated, Hemingway read these obituaries. Jeffrey Meyers recounts how Ernest "studied the obituaries and preserved them in two handsome scrapbooks" (506), behaving a bit like Tom Sawyer getting to look in at his funeral. The author "was, as usual, proud of his ability to endure and survive his wounds," even "jok[ing] . . . that his cracked vertebrae had caused a permanent erection" (505), tying the experience and ordeal to his masculinity and sexual prowess. The degree to which Hemingway was fascinated with those obituaries was perhaps unnatural. In her memoir, Mary wrote of how Ernest "read and read [the premature obituaries] enthralled and gave no attention when I objected that the everlasting reading suggested unseemly egotism" as even "after [their] day's and evening's guests had departed, he read in bed. Then, heeding [Mary's] objections to the light, he read in the bathroom" (1976, 387). While Hemingway might have seen his survival as representing his strength and continued ability to persevere over death, "there is a certain vulnerability . . . in this unique vignette of a man compulsively reading about his own death far into the Nairobi night" (Ondaatje 2003, 204). Though it might look like a man reveling in his own perceived invincibility, perhaps it was Hemingway understanding his own mortality and how suddenly the end might come for him.

These plane crashes, and the nature of Hemingway's injuries from them, hastened Hemingway's physical and mental decline, which ended with him taking his own life. Though "as far as the public knew, Hemingway had proven himself to be indestructible . . . [i]n reality, however, the plane crashes had done irreparable harm" (Kale 2016, 168). Andrew Farah tracks the different concussive injuries Hemingway suffered throughout his life in *Hemingway's Brain*, describing how "the greatest damage occurred" (2017, 35) because of these plane crashes in Africa. Farah goes on to recount how "the second one in particular involved significant traumatic brain injury" and "was his most severe concussive incident to date," as "none of his other accidents had taken such toll, and friends agreed that after the crashes Hemingway was never the same man" (37). Mary Dearborn writes of how "the damage to his head was the most serious," leaving Hemingway with "his fifth major concussion and probably the worst of any of them" (2017, 563).

Though the wounds to his body received the most attention and notice, it was the injury to his brain that would have the greatest impact on the rest of Ernest's life and perhaps contribute most directly to the path that ultimately concluded with his suicide. Dearborn describes how "his brain injury affected him profoundly, reactivating the worst of his mental illness, his mood swinging wildly between mania and depression[; and] his fantasies multiplied[;] . . . [he was] trying out new tall tales [as] discretion and inhibitions, heretofore a check on the worst of his excesses, seem to have all but vanished" (564). Reynolds's assessment is similar and puts an even more pronounced point on it, writing that Hemingway "at fifty-four . . . was in worse physical shape than when he was blown up at eighteen; his aging body was much slower to heal, never again regaining its full power" (*Final Years*, 1999, 274).

Verdict: True.

Were Hemingway and F. Scott Fitzgerald in Love with Each Other?

Thomas Bevilacqua

No other writer is quite as closely linked with Hemingway as F. Scott Fitzgerald. Though, like so many of Hemingway's other relationships, their closeness deteriorated over time, there was a clear connection and affection between the two American authors who defined so much of what we know as the "Lost Generation." Hemingway famously said of Fitzgerald that "his talent was as natural as the pattern that was made by the dust on a butterfly's wings" (2009, 125), commenting on Fitzgerald's innate gift for writing beautiful prose.

The relationship between Hemingway and Scott's wife, Zelda Fitzgerald, could charitably be described as fraught. "When Hemingway met Zelda there was instant mutual antipathy," Matthew Bruccoli recounts. Hemingway "thought she was crazy and told Fitzgerald so . . . believ[ing] that Zelda was jealous of Fitzgerald's work and that she fostered his drinking in order to interfere with his writing" (2002, 226).

Hemingway's distaste for Zelda tended to focus on how she negatively affected Fitzgerald's writing, as Hemingway "could not understand why Fitzgerald remained loyal to Zelda in her madness" (Meyers 1985, 164), Zelda's anger toward Hemingway took on a different quality particularly for his pronounced masculine persona (or perhaps posture), as Zelda referred to Hemingway as "a professional he-man" and "a pansy with hair on his chest" (quoted in Bruccoli 2002, 226), conceiving of Hemingway's outsize masculinity as nothing but a posture and not rooted in anything true or authentic. But perhaps the most notable salvo in this cold war between Zelda and Ernest, and the one that caused the greatest consternation to Scott Fitzgerald, was the idea that Hemingway and Fitzgerald were entangled in an unrequited love affair.

Bruccoli recounts Zelda's "charging that [Scott] was involved in a homosexual liaison with Hemingway, which hurt him more than anything else she said" (275). Scott Donaldson echoes this claim in his biography of Fitzgerald, describing how "Zelda provoked her husband's anger by accusing him of homosexuality . . . outrag[ing] him by naming Ernest Hemingway as the man he loved" (2012, 74). Donaldson notes how "Fitzgerald . . . made a hero out of Hemingway . . . work[ing] with vigor to promote [Hemingway's] career" as he "obviously felt a deep affection for him" (74). This affection was what Zelda was able to fashion into a cudgel to attack her husband, using accusations and insinuations to attack Scott's masculinity and heteronormativity. After "Zelda suffered her mental breakdown and was hospitalized in the spring of 1930 . . . she related the same tale. Her husband was a homosexual, in love with a man named Hemingway," an accusation that led to Fitzgerald wanting to stay away from his wife "until she disabused herself of such notions," as "he was especially troubled by her conviction, which served to make her story more credible" (75).

Zelda's contention of a love affair between Hemingway and Fitzgerald might have emerged, in part, as an act of projection. The 1930 admittance form to the Malmaison outside of Paris, where Zelda was hospitalized, notes that Zelda possessed "some obsessive ideas, the main one of which is her fear of becoming a homosexual. She thinks she is in love with her dance teacher (Madame X) as she had already thought in the past of being in love with another woman" (quoted in Bruccoli, 2002, 274). Hemingway hints at this in *A Moveable Feast*. Of the Fitzgeralds' marriage, Hemingway writes that Zelda had used other men to make Scott jealous but that "she had never made him really jealous with another man since [a French navy pilot]" and that "she was making him jealous with other women" (2009, 155).

Zelda was not the only person to have alleged a romantic entanglement between Hemingway and Fitzgerald. Bruccoli recounts how Robert McAlmon, an American author as well as the owner of the publication house in Paris that published Hemingway's first book *Three Stories and Ten Poems*, "envied the success of Fitzgerald and Hemingway, and later spread gossip about them, culminating in the fabrication that they were homosexual lovers" (2002, 232–33).

While the two men were so close that many would wonder if they were not secretly in love with one another, that relationship would deteriorate over their life. In 1926, Fitzgerald wrote to Hemingway, "I can't tell you how much your friendship has meant to me during this year and a half. It is the brightest thing in our trip to Europe for me" (1995, 148), but once that time in Europe was over, the friendship seemed to dissipate, which does not seem terribly indicative of two men being in love with one another. The deterioration of this relationship began while the two were still living in Paris. Morley Callaghan recounts how after Hemingway moved to a new apartment, he asked, "You didn't tell Scott where I live, did you?" because the Fitzgeralds were liable to "come walking in on us at all hours" (2002, 160).

Scott Donaldson notes that "Fitzgerald and Hemingway were on the same continent during most of the 1930s," with Hemingway decamping to Key West while the Fitzgeralds returned to Montgomery, Alabama, but "nothing came to pass" in terms of their reconnecting, as "the bloom was off their friendship [and] their correspondence trailed off"; "Hemingway became increasingly intolerant and unsympathetic toward his old friend, while Fitzgerald struggled gamely to preserve the illusion of what had once been the closest of relationships" (1999, 161–62). As Hemingway's career and stature grew and the Fitzgerald star continued to fade, Ernest "was unable to generate any sympathy for Fitzgerald . . . kid[ding about] Fitzgerald's troubles with bullying humor" rather than offering true support (Bruccoli 2002, 401). This would play out in print as well, with Hemingway's story "The Snows of Kilimanjaro" featuring "a contemptuous reference to Fitzgerald" that left Fitzgerald "deeply hurt by Hemingway's public betrayal of their friendship" (408–9). After the last time the two were in the same room,[3] when Hemingway was in Hollywood for a screening of *The Spanish Earth*, Fitzgerald reflected in his notebooks, "I talk with the authority of failure—Ernest with the authority of success. We could never sit across the table again" (quoted in Bruccoli 2002, 421). Hemingway's dismissive portrayal of Fitzgerald in *A Moveable Feast*, written years after Fitzgerald's own death, reflects the deterioration of that relationship as well; Hemingway felt that he had to settle scores or dismiss Fitzgerald as a way of better positioning himself.

The alacrity with which the friendship between Fitzgerald and Hemingway diminished does make it seem as though a romantic entanglement between the two was impossible. There was barely enough substance there to sustain a working friendship between two writers.

It is also worth considering that, throughout the biographical record of Hemingway and Fitzgerald, there is no evidence that either man had a sexual relationship with any other man. Thus both men would have been making an exception regarding their sexual preferences for this one instance. Were this to be the case, one would need greater evidence than the accusations of Zelda, a figure who knew just how cutting these claims would be to the two men. But one cannot find that evidence, and thus it stands as another indication that this myth is untrue.

Verdict: False.

Did Hemingway Have an Affair with Josephine Baker?

Thomas Bevilacqua

In addition to stories of big-game hunting and adventure, the Hemingway mythos carries with it an air of romance. As we envision Hemingway the adventurer and the big-game hunter, we also see him as a kind of Don Juan, particularly in his younger years in Lost Generation Paris. We see this time as being especially romantic in a city like Paris, which is inexorably linked with love. So when Hemingway crosses paths with any of the great and famous women of that time, the natural inclination is to assume that they had an affair. One such figure Hemingway was alleged to have an affair with was the actress and entertainer Josephine Baker. But while it would have made for an outstanding story, and Hemingway might have wished it were true as a way of promoting an image of himself, the two did not engage in any kind of romance.

These rumors stem from the fact that both were in Paris during the 1920s, running with much of the same Lost Generation crowd. Josephine Baker was certainly a celebrity and renowned for her great beauty. After performing in New York City, Baker was brought over to Paris by Caroline Dudley to perform in one of her shows. In that show, Baker could be found dancing and performing in just a skirt made of bananas, a costume for which she would become famous and with which she would always be closely associated. Baker was a figure in that cultural milieu of Paris, "fashion[ing] herself as an icon through performance . . . [and] transform[ing] her theatrical performances into social and political statements" by using an "early appeal [that] was based on an exotic performative image that used the primitive, non-Western 'other' as a point of reference and a source of fantasy" (Jules-Rosette 2007, 48–49). Just as writers like Hemingway and James Joyce and Gertrude Stein were pushing the boundaries of what literature could do, Baker was doing something similar in the realm of performance, both on the cabaret stage as well as later in film.

For these reasons, she was a figure who stood out among those living in Paris as the time, including Hemingway. It's also easy to understand why one might think Hemingway had an affair with Baker, as he is quoted as calling the actress "the most sensational woman anyone ever saw . . . or ever will," though the specific attribution of that quote cannot be found (as one sees throughout *Mythbusting Hemingway*, quotes attributed to the author that he did not actually say constitute something of a recurring theme).

However, while they met and interacted, there does not seem to be any evidence that a romantic affair was consummated between the two. Those interactions between Hemingway and Baker are documented in A. E. Hotchner's book *Hemingway in Love*. We must note that Hotchner would have heard these stories from Hemingway more than thirty years after they occurred and during a period in Hemingway's life when he was particularly prone to exaggeration. Hotchner tells us of Hemingway being at Le Jockey in Montparnasse and unable to "take [his] eyes off a beautiful woman on the dance floor" who though "on a very hot night . . . was wearing a black fur coat" (2015, 95). The two did meet on that night, but Hemingway "spent that night with Josephine, sitting at her kitchen table, drinking champagne sent by an admirer . . . carr[ying] on nonstop about [his] trouble, analyzing, explaining, condemning, justifying" as "Josephine listened, intense, sympathetic." Like Hemingway, Josephine was one who "had suffered from double love" (96), which was Hemingway's current state of mind with regard to his feelings about Hadley and Pauline. It seemed to be a very intimate conversation, with discussions of souls and how Hemingway "could convince [his] soul that despite [his] rejection of one of these women and inflicting hurt on her, it shouldn't reject [him]" (97), but nothing romantic transpired between the two during that meeting. Carl Eby also notes that another story Hotchner recounts involving Hemingway and Josephine Baker "bear[s] a more than suspicious resemblance to a passage in Hemingway's heavily autobiographical story, 'The Snows of Kilimanjaro,'" and that story "reeking as it does of the men's locker room and stale detective novels, is surely one of [Hemingway's] lies" (1995, 99) though Eby does "recognize that Baker and Hemingway were friends" (114n1).

Later in her life, Baker performed in London and told stories about her time in Paris: "I started in 1924, and we were all beginners together—Pablo, Matisse, Hemingway. I used to look after them, picking up their clothes, getting them organized" (Baker and Chase 1993, 474), which goes along with Hotchner's insights into the Hemingway-Baker interactions. However, Baker had a tendency (much like Hemingway) to exaggerate and stretch the limits of credulity. As Phyllis Rose notes, the singer "tried on different pasts as though they were dresses, to see which suited her" (1991, 114).

One aspect of Baker's life seems like something out of Hemingway's fiction or something that the author himself would admire in general. Extensively documented in the book *Agent Josephine: American Beauty, French Hero, British Spy* by Damien Lewis, Baker served as a member of the French resistance, reporting to French intelligence on what she would overhear amid her performances, which would often be attended by powerful figures connected to the Axis, in addition to other supporting actions for the cause against the Nazis. When the Germans occupied Paris, she helped support the Free French and later would entertain Allied troops. Baker's desire to help fight against the Nazis is evident particularly after a "bleak 1928 tour of Austria and Germany" where "she'd first come face-to-face with the vile reality of Nazism" (Lewis 2022, 57). For her work, Baker earned the Resistance Medal by the French Committee of National Liberation, the Croix de Guerre, and was named a

Chevalier of the Légion d'Honneur by General Charles de Gaulle. Baker's service as a member of the French resistance was not just a boost to the Allied cause, fighting to stop the encroachment of Fascism across Europe and the rest of the world. It was also a transformative moment for Baker and who she would become. As Lewis writes in the preface to his book, this service "was a watershed moment" for Baker as "before it she had been a glittering and beguiling superstar, blessed with beauty, talent, and an ability to charm and to connect with her audience that few performers have rivalled" but "after the war, . . . she would also take up the cudgels for the battle for freedom and civil liberties in all its forms . . . never forget[ting] the lesson of the war years: freedom must be fought for, every day" (Lewis 2022, xxv).

Verdict: False.

Did Ava Gardner Skinny-Dip in Hemingway's Pool, and Did He Threaten to Fire Anyone Who Drained the Water?

Thomas Bevilacqua

Hemingway struck up many friendships with other celebrities and major figures. The most prominent athletes and bullfighters were among those Hemingway considered to be friends, to the point where there are too many to reasonably mention. Gary Cooper and Ingrid Bergman, who starred in the film adaptation of Hemingway's novel *For Whom the Bell Tolls*, found themselves in the social circle of the author. Marlene Dietrich, a titan of early cinema, was beloved by the writer. Another was actress Ava Gardner. Gardner (who was no stranger to celebrity after having married both Mickey Rooney and Frank Sinatra while also maintaining an ongoing relationship with Howard Hughes) starred in the film adaptations of *The Killers*, *The Snows of Kilimanjaro*, and *The Sun Also Rises*, connecting her with Hemingway in her professional life.

The two connected socially as well. As Gardner described in her autobiography, this was "a happy situation that eventually led to Papa and [she] becoming good chums" (1990, 85). The two wouldn't meet until 1954 when the actress was hospitalized with kidney stones. "Luis Miguel [Dominguin, bullfighter and Gardner's then boyfriend] left the hospital only once . . . and when he did he came back with Papa Hemingway, who [she'd] never met until then," and they "became friends from that moment on" (Gardner 1990, 204). It was clear that knowing Hemingway had a profound effect on the actress. As Michael

Reynolds recounts, the actress stated that "there were only two men she would want with herself on a desert island: Adlai Stevenson . . . and Ernest Hemingway" (*Final Years*, 1999, 281). The Ava Gardner Museum, located in Johnstown County, North Carolina, where the actress was born, has a post on its website titled "The Author and the Actress: Ava Gardner's Friendship with Ernest 'Papa' Hemingway" that speaks to the strong connection between Gardner and Hemingway. It went beyond the mere entangling of two extremely famous (and notorious) people to something more substantial.

One story that persists regarding the Hemingway-Gardner friendship (a relationship that does appear, like his relationship with Marlene Dietrich, to have been chaste) is that during her visit to the Finca Vigía, the actress skinny-dipped in Hemingway's pool, and Hemingway told his staff that the pool was never to be drained. This story appears in sources as diverse as Patrick McDonnell's 2018 article for the *Los Angeles Times*, on the preservation effort at the Hemingways' Cuban abode, and the Difford's cocktail guide's online encyclopedia entry on the actress as a famous imbiber.

In his *Hemingway Log*, Brewster Chamberlin identified the incident as having occurred in August 1954 at the Finca Vigía in Cuba, when Gardner "famously swims nude in the pool" (2015, 294); Andrew Feldman confirms this as he writes that during that time "the Hemingways received visitors at the Finca Vigía, such as Ava Gardner, swimming naked in his pool" (2019, 255). Drawing on one of Hemingway's African journals housed at the JFK Library, Timothy Christian corroborates: "Ava Gardner came to Havana . . . went fishing with Ernest and Mary on *Pilar* and came to lunch at the Finca, following which, according to René [Villarreal], Ava swam nude in the pool" (2022, 230–31). Villarreal, the majordomo of the Finca Vigía, recalled in his memoir that during Gardner's visit, he noticed a "group of young boys jumping the fence and making their way up to the house. When they got close to the pool, they hid behind trees" as "Gardner was swimming nude in the cool waters of the pool" (98). Valerie Hemingway, without mentioning anything about what the actress was or was not wearing when she swam, remembers that "Ava Gardner . . . had lunched at the *finca*, swum in its pool, and joined the Hemingways in downtown Havana for drinks and dinner at El Floridita" (2005, 96).

The fact that Gardner swam, likely nude, in Hemingway's pool appears across so wide a range of sources that it appears to be true, and it also makes sense given Gardner's noted willingness to do what she wanted, which stemmed from the strength and individuality she possessed. The question of Hemingway's response to this, telling his staff that they should not drain the pool, is a bit more complicated. None of the major works on Hemingway records evidence that he said that the pool was not to be drained. However, Norberto Fuentes, a Cuban writer and journalist, recounts an exchange that occurred in the 1950s between the author and neighbors who "decided to drop in on Hemingway." When the author "received them at the swimming pool," Hemingway told them, "Please remove your shoes and dip your feet reverently in the water of this pool, where Ava Gardner swam naked his morning" (1984, 68). Though that is not the same as saying to not drain the water, it does reflect a reverence for the pool in which the beautiful Gardner swam.

Verdict: Probable.

Did Hemingway's Mother Dress Him Like a Girl?

Thomas Bevilacqua

For an author who has become an icon of big and bold masculinity, it might come as surprise to some that Ernest Hemingway dressed in clothes meant for the opposite gender. But that was the case. Specifically, as a very young child, he was dressed in clothing meant for girls, and it occurred for a very specific reason.

Hemingway's mother, Grace Hall Hemingway, wanted to have twins. When that did not happen organically, Grace made it happen by dressing Ernest and his older sister Marcelline as twins. In her memoir, Marcelline says, "Mother often told me she had always wanted twins. and that though I was a little over a year older than Ernest . . . she was determined to have us be as much like twins as possible. When we were little, Ernest and I were dressed alike in various out fits. . . . We wore our hair exactly alike in bangs in a square-cut Dutch bob" (Sanford 1962, 61). One can find pictures of the three- or four-year-old Ernest wearing an outfit that one would expect to see on a girl, with Grace labeling him "summer girl" in pictures she collected in baby books.

Dressing boys like girls "until they were old enough to walk" (Lynn, 1995, 38) was common when Hemingway was a child. As Hemingway biographer Kenneth Lynn notes, "There was a much greater variety of appearance among little boys" at that time. It was "an age of innocence about infantile sexuality, the average mother felt less constrained in making choices about this matter than her modern counterpart would" (1995, 38).

"The practice was an expression of a general sentimentaliza-tion of childhood," Dearborn writes, "wherein innocence—associ-ated with what was thought to be the gentle, fairer sex—was highly prized" (2017, 22). While this practice was common for one-year-old boys and girls in "a world of Victorian values, Protestant ethics, and middle-class comforts" (Kale 2016, 11) where Ernest began his life, Grace Hemingway's decision to continue doing this well beyond that age was perhaps a bit extreme. The baby book that Grace kept for her son, now housed at the John F. Kennedy Library in Boston, even documents the young Ernest's concern that Santa Claus would not know that he was actually a boy and thus he would not receive the appropriate presents. Lynn determined that "no more than 10 or 15 percent" of those boys "were still kept in girls' clothes until they were four or five years old" (1995, 39). Hemingway's mother even "[held] Marcelline back so that she and Ernest might enter first grade together" as a way of continuing the illusion that they were twins (Donaldson 1999, 190). Along with an envelope containing the young Hemingway's clippings from a haircut, Grace wrote, "Ernest Miller Hemingway, hair cut off Feb 15th 1906, he can never wear long hair again[4] as he is 6 ½ yrs and in school. My precious boy. A 'real' boy" (quoted in Lynn 1995, 45). In her memoir, Marcelline is sure to note that this went on for an extreme amount of time. She describes how Grace "continued with her plan . . . even into our school life" and that "there were times, especially in school, when [she] would have liked to go ahead by [herself]" (Sanford 1962, 62). One can certainly imagine Ernest feeling the same way.

Though one hesitates to play armchair psychologist, one can certainly draw a line between this decision by Hemingway's mother and the predilections that appeared in Hemingway's writing and his personal life. Carl Eby concurs with this idea, writing how Grace Hemingway, in "shifting [Ernest] between 'boyish and 'girlish' cos-tumes and continually playing with his appearance . . . , sent pro-foundly ambiguous and conflicting signals to her young son. At times she clearly thought of him as a 'girl'" (1998, 97). Within

Hemingway's fiction, *The Garden of Eden* is replete with mentions of the interchangeability between David and Catherine Bourne as they make themselves look like one another, and display a fluidity regarding their roles in their bedroom activities. In addition to the acts of twinning and matching hairstyles,[5] there were also moments when Catherine, in the fluid interchange of shifting sexual identity and behavior, dresses in a way that when the novel was set would have been much more typical of a man rather than a woman. When one encounters these moments in Hemingway's fiction (and they are hardly confined to *The Garden of Eden*), one cannot help but imagine that this choice by his mother perhaps planted seeds that would manifest themselves later in life. Hemingway experimented with reversing gender roles to various degrees in each of his four marriages. Later in life, he referred to himself as Mary's "girl" and periodically called himself "Catherine" or "Kathrine." Mary, in turn, was his "kitten brother" in their gender swap fantasies.

Verdict: True.

Did Hemingway Meet Benito Mussolini?

Thomas Bevilacqua

There has been a great deal of attention paid to Hemingway's inter-actions with celebrities, including in this very book.[6] But it was not just the stars of the screen and sporting arenas with whom Heming-way engaged. The author found himself in the halls of political power, sharing rooms with those who shaped world historical events. Hemingway met then president Franklin Delano Roosevelt when he, along with Martha Gellhorn and Jorie Ivens, traveled to the White House for a screening of their documentary film *The Spanish Earth*. While that documentary focused on depicting the fascist threat emerging in Spain in the 1930s, earlier in his life Hemingway met one of the major figures in the establishment of Fascism in Europe in the early twentieth century—Benito Mussolini.

In 1922, Hemingway returned to Italy, the country in which he had been wounded during the First World War and that had intro-duced him to a world of violence and chaos. While in Milan, showing Hadley around the city, an attack led by Italian Fascists occurred in Bologna. Mussolini, the leader of the Fascist movement in Italy, was in Milan at the same time as Hemingway after this attack occurred. Hemingway took time from "holding hands under the table and drinking Capri with fresh peaches and strawberries" with Hadley to "arrange an interview" with the future dictator "in the editor's office of the *Popolo d'Italia*" (Baker 1969, 93).

Hemingway recounted the meeting between him and the Ital-ian in the June 24, 1922, edition of the *Toronto Star*. The opening paragraph of that story sets quite an impressive scene. Hemingway describes Mussolini "sit[ting] at his desk at the fuse of the great powder magazine that he has laid through all Northern and Central Europe . . . occasionally fondl[ing] the ears of a wolfhound pup, looking like a short-eared jackrabbit, that plays with the papers on the floor beside the big desk" (Hemingway, *Sun Also Rises & Other Writings*, 2020, 38). Hemingway's piece goes on to describe Mussolini's life and rise to power, closing by asking this question: "What does Mussolini, sitting at his desk in the office of the *Popolo d'Italia* and fondling the ears of his wolfhound pup, intend to do with his 'political party organized as a military force'?" (40). One can infer in Hemingway's reportage his concern with the rising presence of Fascism in Europe, which manifested itself in his writing during the Spanish Civil War and World War II. Hemingway saw that "Mussolini sat at the fuse of a powder keg" and "the question in Ernest's mind was what he would do with his matches" (Baker 1969, 93).

This would not be the last time that Hemingway wrote about the Italian dictator for the *Toronto Star*. Hemingway filed the story headlined "Mussolini, Europe's Prize Bluffer More Like Bottomley than Napoleon" on January 27, 1923. In that piece of reporting, Hemingway recounts how the dictator "would receive the press," where they would find Mussolini "his face contorted into the famous frown . . . absorbed in his book" which was "a French-English dictionary—held upside down" (1967, 64). Hemingway makes it clear through this detail that he can see through the bluster and pomposity of Mussolini, identifying him as "the biggest bluff in Europe. If Mussolini would have me taken out and shot tomorrow morning I would still regard him as a bluff," and there was "the weakness in his mouth which forces him to scowl the famous Mussolini scowl that is imitated by every 19 year old Fascisto in Italy" (64). But while Hemingway may have noticed the weakness in Mussolini, he also recognized that which the dictator could accomplish with his ability "to rattle the saber against a foreign country to make his patriots forget their dissatisfaction at home in their flaming zeal to be at the throats of the enemy"—in that instance, Ethiopia (207).

Mussolini also made a brief appearance in Hemingway's fiction in a story that depicts the presence of Fascism in Italy in those years that would culminate in World War II. In the short story "Che Ti Dice La Patria?"[7] Hemingway describes how in Spezia, Italy, "on the walls of the houses were stenciled eye-bugging portraits of Mussolini, with hand-painted 'vivas,' the double V in black paint with drippings of paint down the side" (*Short Stories*, 2003, 292–93) while the narrator, who is sitting down for dinner at a restaurant, mentions how "Mussolini has abolished the brothels" (294).

Verdict: True.

Was Hemingway Friends
with Fidel Castro?

Thomas Bevilacqua

The period of Hemingway's life in which he spent time in Cuba also happened to coincide with one of the major moments in Cuban history—the deposing of Fulgencio Batista and the installation of Fidel Castro as the leader of the country, which was a position he held for more than five decades. Because of the proximity of Castro's ascension to power to the time when Hemingway was most closely tied to Cuba, the idea that the two figures were friends began to circulate. We know that Hemingway spent time in the presence of other world leaders,[8] and the idea that the revolutionary head of Cuba would be friends with the man who revolutionized literature was too good to overlook. Sadly, the truth is much less interesting. The two did meet, but it was only in passing, and no pronounced relationship emerged from their crossing paths.

The meeting between the two men occurred after Hemingway "invited [Castro] and Che Guevara to go fishing" specifically at "the annual Hemingway Marlin Fishing Tournament" (Feldman 2019, 332). On May 15, 1960, the Cuban communist leader attended that very fishing tournament which bore Hemingway's name and over which he presided. As Timothy Christian describes it, "Mary and the others watched Fidel's boat through binoculars, and on the first day, they saw him catch two marlins, both according to the big-game fishing rules. The next day, he caught a third marlin, and the combined weight of his three fish won first prize—Ernest's silver trophy" (2022, 273). Andrew Feldman writes of Castro's "stroke of beginner's luck" when it came to fishing and that he "took the silver trophy cup, which the writer presented him that evening at the dock" before "Hemingway and Castro conversed for about thirty minutes somewhat separated from the rest of the crowd" (2019, 333).

The moment of Hemingway shaking Castro's hand after his victory was immortalized in a photograph for *Life* in 1960. The conversation between the two was cordial, as "they chatted about fishing" and "Castro said he'd read *For Whom the Bell Tolls* and had used its ideas about guerrilla warfare in his battles in the Sierra Maestra"[9] (Christian 2022, 273). In his spoken autobiography, Castro says that he would "have liked to know Hemingway better" though he "was able to talk to him twice, quite briefly" (2007, 592). It is interesting to note that Castro recalled that the two met twice, rather than the single time that has been recorded in much of the history surrounding Hemingway and Castro. Did the Cuban dictator's memory fail him? Was there a second meeting between the two men that no one knows about? In any event, Castro's words in that autobiography reflect the less-than-exciting nature of their relationship.

Though his interactions with Castro himself were straightforward (they were acquaintances but never truly friends), Hemingway's relationship with Castro's cause and regime is a bit more complicated but also more interesting to examine. Robert Wheeler, in his book *Hemingway's Havana: A Reflection of the Writer's Life in Cuba*, notes how in the writer's life and writing, there was "an unwavering support for the downtrodden—a support that later reemerged in Castro's Cuban Revolution" (2018, 106). Even if these two men could not be understood as being actual friends, certain shared concerns and ethical beliefs bind the two men together in the minds of many. Hemingway even "wish[ed] Castro all luck" as he thought "the Cuban people now have a decent chance for the first time ever" (Baker 1969, 543).

While Hemingway might have shared certain views and beliefs with those fighting out from under the Batista regime, he also kept his distance from that revolutionary impulse. As the majordomo of the Finca Vigía, René Villarreal, recounted the time amid the Cuban revolution when "Hemingway set out in the *Pilar* with Gregorio [Fuentes, his first mate on the *Pilar*] and tossed overboard a few firearms he stored in the boat[,] . . . he seemed relieved to have gotten rid of the weapons. He didn't want either side getting ahold of them. . . . Papa said that he was too old and too tired to be a part of any of it" (2009, 124). While in earlier days, Hemingway, younger and in better health, might have been inclined to involve himself in some capacity with Castro's claiming of power, those days had passed Hemingway by at that point in his life. Mary Dearborn concludes that Hemingway "felt that disposing of the weapons, taking them out of circulation, meant that fewer people would be hurt or killed with them come the revolution" (2017, 593). Yet the news that Castro had seized power was something that Hemingway found "delightful" and said so to a *New York Times* reporter, though "Mary got him to call the reporter back and change the quote to say he was 'hopeful'" (593).

After Hemingway's suicide, René Villarreal recounted how "Castro met with Mary at the *Finca* [as] she explained her wishes to donate the house to the Cuban people in exchange for being permitted to take the remaining artwork and valuables out of the country" but Castro "left without giving her a response" (2009, 141) before "the Cuban Ministry of Culture finally agreed to Mary's request and allowed her to take the artwork and personal mementos" along with Hemingway's literary manuscripts (143). One cannot help but think that if Castro and Hemingway had been friends, as history would like us to believe, these impediments would not have occurred, and there would not have been such delays.

Verdict: False.

Did Hemingway Say, "We Are All Broken; That's How the Light Gets In"?

Thomas Bevilacqua

As he has become a myth or brand unto himself, there has arisen a whole industry devoted to products featuring a quotation attributed to Ernest Hemingway. It feels like there are more examples of this than with perhaps any other writer short of, perhaps, William Shakespeare. However, many of the quotes emblazoned upon notebooks and coffee mugs and pint glasses and countless other products were never actually uttered by the author. One example of a quote improperly attributed to Hemingway is "We are all broken. That's how the light gets in." One can conceive of why this is thought to be something Hemingway said, as it both reflects ideas with which Hemingway engaged and things that he wrote. But even though these elements are present in the quotation, it was not actually uttered by the writer.

Perhaps the simplest explanation for this quote being identified as coming from Hemingway stems from a passage in Hemingway's novel *A Farewell to Arms*: "The world breaks everyone and afterward many are strong at the broken places. But those that will not break it kills. It kills the very good and the very gentle and the very brave impartially. If you are none of these you can be sure it will kill you too but there will be no special hurry" (1995, 249). Breaking and wounding are major parts of Hemingway's writing. They are the themes and tropes to which he returned throughout his writing career. But the specific phrasing about being broken and light getting in did not come from Hemingway.

A more accurate source of this quote is the musician and author Leonard Cohen, as it reads like a slight rephrasing of a line in his song "Anthem"—"There is a crack, a crack in everything. That's how the light gets in." That line from Cohen's song is likely the source of the quote as it entered the popular imagination. Quote Investigator, a website devoted to tracking down the sources for famous quotations and determining their veracity, also points to lines written by Ralph Waldo Emerson as providing this oft-circulated aphorism. But Quote Investigator concludes "that this quotation was not crafted by Ernest Hemingway . . . hypothesiz[ing] that the 1929 statement by Hemingway [in *A Farewell to Arms*] and the 1992 lyric by Leonard Cohen both strongly influenced the evolution of the expression and its ascription."

Verdict: False.

Was Hemingway Friends with Marlene Dietrich?

Thomas Bevilacqua

As one of the great figures in American life in the early years of the twentieth century, Ernest Hemingway spent time traveling in the circles of other famous and notorious people. One of those celebrities with whom he became acquainted was the famous actress Marlene Dietrich, whose career spanned the silent era to the later decades of the twentieth century. Hemingway considered the great German-born beauty a true friend, creating a fascinating pairing of two titans of early twentieth-century culture.

The two first met while traveling, though the conventional wisdom that the meeting occurred in March 1934 is incorrect. By this point, Dietrich had moved from her native Germany to the United States and was established as a Hollywood film star based on her work in Josef von Sternberg films such as *Morocco* and *Shanghai Express*. Carlos Baker and Mary Dearborn, among other biographers, concluded that this meeting between Hemingway and Dietrich occurred on the *Île de France*. Paul Hendrickson investigated the newspaper accounts of the SS *Paris*'s arrival in the United States (2011, 475) and determined that it was the boat on which they were traveling. Dearborn recounts how "legend has it that the actress was joining a party in the dining room when she saw that she would be the thirteenth member of the party. Superstitious, she said she had to decline, but Hemingway stepped forward and said he would be the thirteenth[. . . . This was] the beginning of a lifelong friendship" (2017, 336). Sandra Spanier said that the fact "that Hemingway and

Dietrich would meet aboard a luxury liner crossing the Atlantic at the same time they were featured in the same issue of *Vanity Fair*[10] is a wonderful story. Except it is not true" (Spanier 2020, 94). Katie Warczak, through archival research as part of the Hemingway Letters project, supports Spanier's assertion and identifies "Dietrich's and Hemingway's first encounter" as having "happened aboard the *Normandie* during its 19 to 24 November 1938 crossing from Le Havre, France, to New York," as it was "the earliest date Hemingway Letters Project researchers could confirm their meeting" (2020, 99).

After that initial meeting, the two connected again in 1944 as "Dietrich had by now become another member of [Ernest's] stable of beautiful celebrities [which] included Ingrid Bergman and would expand to accommodate Ava Gardner and the socialite Slim Hayward" (Dearborn 2017, 470). Dearborn describes how despite "Ernest profess[ing] his undying love" to these beautiful women, "they evidently chose not to notice his sexual attentions . . . [and while] drawn to Ernest by his charisma and charm, none of them seems to have wanted to sleep with him" (470).

Hemingway's letters to the actress did seem to reflect feelings of something like romantic love on behalf of Hemingway, feelings not reciprocated by Dietrich or ever acted upon. One such letter, in which Hemingway makes grand overtures to the beautiful Dietrich, was auctioned off in 2017. Hemingway's correspondence with Dietrich featured writing "indistinguishable from love letters, yet the relationship" with the woman he affectionally would refer to as Daughter "remained platonic" (Dearborn 2017, 470). Interviewed regarding the auction of that letter, Hemingway Letters project general editor Sandra Spanier recounted how the relationship between the two was "platonic" and that "[t]hey claimed the timing was never right for the two of them to get together, but they were very intimate friends" (quoted in Birnbaum 2017). The intimacy Hemingway felt with Dietrich manifested itself in the way in which he would confide in her, as "Hemingway was rarely candid or introspective among his male friends" but specifically with Dietrich he "was comfortable talking . . . about his personal demons" (Hutchisson 2016, 90). The correspondence between the two reflects this as well, as Hemingway confided in Dietrich on matters both literary (sharing a section of what would become *Islands in the Stream*) and personal (confiding in the actress about his family-related worries, specifically as they pertained to his children). In some regard, the relationship between Hemingway and Dietrich sounds like what transpired between the author and Josephine Baker. There was a great deal of intimacy, yet the relationship never moved into the realm of the romantic. Mary Welsh Hemingway even recounts a time when "Marlene used to wander down to Ernest's room to sit on his bathtub and sing to him while he shaved" (1976, 128). Throughout her autobiography, Mary refers to Dietrich in a friendly and appreciative manner, which also seems to indicate that the relationship between Ernest and Marlene was not romantic in nature.

Verdict: True.

Did Hemingway Fight in World War I?

Thomas Bevilacqua

Just as it was for the entire world, World War I was an important event for Hemingway. It would not be much of a shock for someone to have an image of Hemingway fighting in that war, given his age at the time the war broke out. An eighteen-year-old Hemingway, charging through enemy territory to beat back the advancing German army, certainly fits with the popular conception of the author.[11]

In addition to how it fit into our collective, myth-addled view of Hemingway as some kind of hypermasculine idol, so much of Hemingway's writing engages with some aspect of World War I, and the characters with which Hemingway is associated are frequently veterans of that conflict in some capacity or another. Nick Adams, Jake Barnes, and Frederic Henry—three of Hemingway's famous protagonists—all served in some capacity in the First World War. In one of the vignettes from *In Our Time*, Hemingway describes Nick Adams as he "sat against the wall of the church where they had dragged him to be clear of machine gun fire in the street[,] . . . hit in the spine" as "stretcher bearers would be along any time now" (*Sun Also Rises & Other Writings*, 2020, 201). Hemingway's first real entry into the literary world would feature pieces like that or like "Soldier's Home," narratives that seemingly reflected one's experience fighting and serving during the First World War as well as the consequences of that service when the fighting had ended. Yet while his experience during World War I, experience that certainly brought him very close to the fighting, was vital to the creation of Hemingway's characters and factors into the fiction he created, it was not in a combat capacity. Hemingway did not actually "fight" in that conflict.

The call of the war, the potential for heroism and bravery, entranced the young Hemingway as it did so many men of that time. "He saw the way the girls turned their heads after uniforms," Michael Reynolds notes. "[H]e listened to parents puff with pride over their solider boys. Somehow he was going to get to the war . . . [and] return, of course, all decorated to Oak Park" (*Young Hemingway*, 1999, 15). Later in his life, Hemingway noted that some of the narratives of the war swept him up and gave him that desire to go overseas and fight. Hemingway recounted how he "was an awful dope when" he traveled to Europe "thinking that we were the home team and the Austrians were the visiting team" (quoted in Baker 1969, 38). Hemingway makes it clear in a letter to Maxwell Perkins that "it was the writers in the last war who wrote propaganda that finished themselves off that way" (Hemingway 1996, 318), reflecting on how these writers made the conflict feel "like the greatest game in the world" (Baker 1969, 38). Reading Hemingway's reflection on what made fighting in the Great War seem like such an enticing option, one cannot help but think of the popular song of the time, George M. Cohan's "Over There," with lines like "Johnnie, get your gun/Get your gun, get your gun/Johnnie show the Hun/Who's a son of a gun/Hoist the flag and let her fly/Yankee Doodle do or die." One can imagine Hemingway, all of eighteen years of age, swept up in the sentiment crystallized in that song and badly wanting to join the fight.

However, the path to the glory and decoration that young Ernest desired proved to be much more difficult than he anticipated. Hemingway attempted to enlist in the US Army but "failed optical tests" which "prevented [his] acceptance in the US military" (Paul 2017, 105). In his quest to find a different route to Europe, he turned to "The Missouri Guard . . . a temporary force authorized by the governor to operate until the return of the National Guard" which allowed "Hemingway, poor eyesight notwithstanding, [to] become a soldier, albeit temporary and unable to serve in Europe" (Florczyk 2014, 18). Though it "offered Hemingway a rudimentary military experience as well as an introduction to ideals motivating participants in the Great War" (19), this ultimately was not going to be sustainable, and he "continued . . . searching for a unit that would send him overseas" (20). Hemingway turned to "enlisting in the ambulance service" as "a whole plausible way to serve," as per the suggestion of Ted Brumback, a friend of Hemingway's when he was in Kansas City working for the *Kansas City Star* (Paul 2017, 105). In his biography of Hemingway's fellow author (and sometime friend) John Dos Passos, Townsend Ludington writes of the (eventual) author of *The U.S.A. Trilogy* "prepar[ing] to sail for the war as an ambulance driver . . . the role in the war of a remarkable number of Americans who later became significant literary figures" including Hemingway (1980, 123). Ludington also recounts how "just before being released from duty" Dos Passos "crossed paths briefly with Ernest Hemingway, who had just arrived at Schio with Section 4 of the Red Cross ambulance" (159).

Though he was not there to participate in the fighting, Hemingway's desire for the action was still present. Brumback noted that "[w]hen [they] arrived in Paris the Germans were shelling the capital [and] . . . Hemingway was as excited as if he'd been sent on general assignment to cover the biggest story of the year" (quoted in Paul 2017, 147). However, the work of ambulance driving did not provide Hemingway with much excitement of war and left him seeking more opportunities to experience the adrenaline rush and brushes with danger he clearly desired. James McGrath Morris writes of how "Hemingway found work as a driver dull. Except for one hairpin turn on the dirt road leading to the front, the infrequent trips to fetch soldiers in need of medical care were boring" (2017, 51). In *Death in the Afternoon*, Hemingway describes "arriving where the munition plant had been" and being "ordered to search the immediate vicinity and surrounding fields for bodies" as they created "an improvised mortuary" (136). Tasks such as these did not provide Hemingway with the opportunity to achieve the kind of glory and heroism he envisioned back in the United States.

An opportunity arose as "men were needed to run emergency canteen operations for soldiers at the Piave front [in Italy], where the battles and the shelling had become fierce" (Paul 2017, 152). It was clear that the fighting in Fossalta, the town out of which Hemingway was based for the canteen service, was seeing its share of the conflict, as Paul writes of "the soggy landscape [that] was littered with the bodies of Austrian soldiers, evidence of the Italians' brutal rebuff of the enemy's charge" (152). As part of the canteen service, Hemingway ventured to the front itself to deliver coffee, cigarettes, mail, chocolate, and other things to Italian soldiers, though doing so on a bicycle rather than in anything like an ambulance. It was doing this work, not fighting, around midnight July 8, 1918, that Hemingway suffered the great wounding that would determine so much of his life and dictate many of the concerns of his literary career.

Verdict: False.

Was Hemingway a Warmonger?

Thomas Bevilacqua

Much of Hemingway's writing depicts scenes of violence and war, narratives filled with soldiers and veterans. With all of that, one could be forgiven for thinking that Hemingway was someone who thought war was somehow a good thing, that he relished and approved of armed combat. However, while Hemingway made war and its aftermath the subject of his writing, his attitudes toward war were certainly critical, and he cannot be understood as a warmonger.

The young Hemingway, like all the young men of the time, was seduced by the promise of glory and heroism in World War I that sent him off to Europe as soon as he could go (though, as discussed elsewhere, not to fight as a soldier but to drive in the ambulance corps).[12] Jeffrey Meyers notes how he was "in high spirits just before he left for Europe" (1985, 27), reflecting the excitement a young man might feel as he prepared to enter the great proving ground of war. But after his experience during the war, namely, his wounding while working in the canteen service at the front, Hemingway's perspective on war and conflict was changed. He later acknowledged the degree to which propaganda and patriotism-driven appeals made him want to seek out service during the war.

Hemingway's skepticism for war appears in much of his fiction. As Frederic Henry thinks in *A Farewell to Arms*, "I was always embarrassed by the words sacred, glorious, and sacrifice and the expression in vain. We had heard them, sometimes standing in the rain almost out of earshot, so that only the shouted words came through, and had read them on proclamations that were slapped up by billposters over other proclamations, now for a long time, and I had seen nothing sacred, and the things that were glorious had no glory and the sacrifices were like the stock yards at Chicago if nothing was done with the meat except to bury it" (1995, 161). It is hard to imagine that someone who relished the thought of warfare and thought it was somehow a good thing could write a passage such as this.

Hemingway's questioning of the language used to discuss war continued into his nonfiction writing. In his 1935 essay "Notes on the Next War" for *Esquire* magazine, Hemingway noted, "They wrote in the old days that it is sweet and fitting to die for one's country. But in modern war there is nothing sweet nor fitting in your dying. You will die like a dog for no good reason" (1967, 209). Hemingway takes the same stance as the poet Wilfred Owen. Owen, a British soldier who died in the final days of the first World War, wrote the poem "Dulce et Decorum Est" that calls out the fiction peddled that there is virtue or dignity that comes along with dying for one's country on the field of battle. Those misguided notions of honor and virtue that lead so many into conflict (and frequently death) have been proven to be flawed and not substantial. "Before the war you always think that it's not you that dies," Hemingway wrote later in that same essay, "but you will die, brother, if you go to it long enough" (1967, 210). As a younger man, Hemingway seemed drawn not, perhaps, by the idea of nobility but rather out of a sense of adventure. Steve Paul notes how the young Hemingway's friend, Ted Brumback, recounted "another memory of his bomb-shelled stint in France" (2017, 106) that "gave a strong picture of the kind of experience Hemingway might expect as he headed to the Italian front in the coming months . . . fac[ing] death[,] . . . surviv[ing] the gas and the relentless downpour of shells" (111). Paul's biography of the young Hemingway notes how his work for the *Kansas City Star* provides "a close-up view of patriotism in wartime and of the impulse . . . that sends a soldier eagerly into the fray" (121). What becomes clear in Hemingway's more mature writing is that he came to see the true carnage that war brought into the world. Hemingway's wounding while on that

Italian front, as well as the wisdom that maturity affords, certainly played a role in that realization, and Hemingway was disabused of idealistic notions of warfare and conflict.

Michael Reynolds recounts how, before the attack on Pearl Harbor pulled the United States into World War II, Hemingway, in a piece for *Esquire*, outlined how "a European war was brewing in which America should play no part." He wrote that "the disillusioned Hemingway[,] . . . the young man sucked in by propaganda during World War I" and further hurt during the Spanish Civil War "when fascism triumphed while democracies refused to help[,] . . . if the war came to him . . . would fight to save his homeland and his people, but never to save the politicians who started the war" (*Final Years*, 1999, 22–23). These are certainly not the views of a true warmonger.

What makes Hemingway's views on warfare so fascinating to consider is that they do not exist in binaries. To be certain, Hemingway was not one who somehow celebrated warfare, yet he also understood, in the world as it was, that it might be necessary. Hemingway articulates this idea more completely in his foreword to the *Treasury for the Free World* anthology, edited by Ben Raeburn and published in the aftermath of World War II after the defeat of global Fascism. In that foreword, Hemingway writes, "Never think that war, no matter how necessary, nor how justified, is not a crime" (1946, xv). There can be reasons war occurs, but that does not in any way diminish its horrific cost. These are hardly the words of someone who would celebrate warfare or want to see more of it occur. We can see this nuance in *For Whom the Bell Tolls*, which reflects how, in Hemingway's worldview, there is the space for evils and wrongs that must be addressed with military force. Yet, as we also see in that novel, Hemingway does not shy away from acknowledging the atrocities and destruction that occur during a conflict, including those committed by the side ostensibly in the right. In that novel of the Spanish Civil War, Hemingway depicts the violent actions undertaken by the loyalists in an unflinching and clear-eyed way that does not diminish their destructive and awful cost while also acknowledging their necessity. What Hemingway always seems to acknowledge is that even though war might be the only recourse, as it was when it came to combating the forces of Hitler and Mussolini, necessity does not mean it is a good or moral thing. *For Whom the Bell Tolls* is a good example of this thinking, as Robert Jordan is a reluctant fighter against the Spanish forces of Franco. Though he knows the nobility of the cause for which he fights, he's not participating in this conflict because he enjoys the fighting. Philip Young observes that "[t]o Jordan there is nothing black and white about his enemies and his friends. . . . The most barbaric atrocity in the novel is perpetrated by his friends" (1981, 105). Jordan thinks, as he prepares to meet his demise at the end of the novel, about how "[t]he world is a fine place and worth the fighting for" (*For Whom the Bell Tolls*, 1995, 467). That quote gets at Hemingway's views on warfare—they are not good unto themselves and are a kind of sacrifice, but for the right cause, they might be what is necessary.

Verdict: False.

Did Hemingway Say That One Should "Write Drunk, Edit Sober"?

Thomas Bevilacqua and Robert K. Elder

The "attributed to Ernest Hemingway" quote industry is a thriving one. In this book, we've attempted to address the misattribution of multiple quotes to Hemingway—those things that sound like something the author might say but where there is no discernible proof he did and there are enough questions about the source of the quote that it's clear it did not come from him. One of those quotes associated with the author is "write drunk, edit sober." It's one you'll see emblazoned on the walls of literary-inclined bars and restaurants and that you might hear repeated by a writer just before they pick up the next round. That construction, to write one way and edit another, has entered the lexicon. It is a framework and a phrasing that screenwriter and director Paul Schrader references, describing how he would "write stoned and revise sober" (quoted in Biskind 1998, 382). However, there is no evidence that Hemingway himself said this. In fact, much of what Hemingway said about drinking and writing contradicts this quote.

In a 1961 interview with Edward Stafford (published in 1964), Hemingway said something that would contradict the first part of that "equation." When Stafford's wife commented to Hemingway that she'd heard he drank heartily before writing, the author replied, "Have you ever heard of anyone who drank while he worked? You're thinking of Faulkner. He does sometimes—and I can tell right in the middle of a page when he's had his first one" (quoted in Stafford). Given the disdain that Hemingway shows for the prospect of drinking while writing, it seems unlikely that he would have said something that seemed to endorse that notion. Hemingway scholar Verna Kale points to the "ample evidence that he just didn't write while drunk!" She continues: "His letters give every indication that he got up early, wrote, and then had lunch and went fishing or shooting or wrote letters. Drinking happened in the afternoons and evenings after the writing was done. Even in *A Moveable Feast*, where he writes about having rum while writing, he isn't drunk—it's just a way to take up space in the cafe where he is working."

Both Quote Investigator and *Writer's Digest* crafted posts aimed at addressing this misattributed quote, trying to determine where exactly it came from. The post on Quote Investigator posits that "[t]he earliest strong match . . . appeared in the 1964 novel 'Reuben, Reuben' by the humorist Peter De Vries which included a character named Gowan McGland whose behaviors and eccentricities were partially modeled on the celebrated Welsh poet Dylan Thomas." Thomas, much like Hemingway, is a literary figure quite closely linked to his propensity to drink; thus a figure modeled on him would be likely to say something like that. The Quote Investigator article goes on to note how that phrasing occurs in the words of Charles Bukowski and the discourse surrounding F. Scott Fitzgerald. It appears as though any writer who is known for enjoying alcoholic beverages is believed to have uttered this quote, which certainly includes Hemingway. Yet when one digs deeper into Hemingway and learns about his practices and preferences, one finds that they so thoroughly contradict the sentiment of that quotation as to make it impossible for him to have uttered it.

Verdict: False.

Was Hemingway *Very* Particular about Hair?

Thomas Bevilacqua

In *Hemingway's Boat: Everything He Loved in Life, and Lost*, Paul Hendrickson writes, "You can't read Ernest Hemingway even half-seriously without becoming aware of his fixation with hair" (363). It was an object of fixation for Hemingway throughout his life, both in his personal life as well as his work, what Mary Dearborn describes as "a fascination with hair—its color, its texture, its length—that became nothing less than an erotic fetish in the grown man" (2017, 24). Dearborn also recounts how "just writing about the shades of hair color would become almost unbearably exciting to him; he would catalogue them with obvious erotic pleasure" (2017, 329). While the idea that someone like Hemingway could have this profound and pronounced fetish regarding, of all things, hair, might seem improbable, yet this is certainly and verifiably true.

Hair plays a prominent role in Hemingway's literary work, perhaps most famously in the posthumously published *The Garden of Eden*, starting in the novel's opening chapter. Catherine Bourne, the wife of protagonist David Bourne, returns one day with "[h]er hair . . . cropped a short as a boy's . . . cut with no compromises . . . bruised back, heavy as always, but the sides were cut short and the ears that grew close to her head were clear and the tawny line of her hair was cropped close to her head and smooth and sweeping back" (1986, 14–15). It is this choice regarding one's hair, how it is worn, that initiates the plot of Hemingway's novel and its exploration of gender norms and ideas of sexuality. It all begins with the hair, and the choices David and Catherine make regarding that hair, which speaks to the importance Hemingway placed upon it.

Hemingway's fascination with hair and its cutting appears in one of his earlier short stories, "Cat in the Rain." In that story, which was collected in *In Our Time*, George's wife asks, "Don't you think it would be a good idea if I let my hair grow out?" and then, "I want to pull my hair back tight and smooth and make a big knot at the back that I can feel," followed by "If I can't have long hair or any fun, I can have a cat" (*Sun Also Rises & Other Writings*, 2020, 229). Throughout his career, Hemingway has his characters change the length and color of their hair (or discuss it) as a way of indirectly having conversations about sexuality, gender, relationships, and identity.

Beyond playing this role in his fiction, this predilection extended into Hemingway's personal life, as he was very concerned with hair, whether it be his own or that of his partner. This concern with hair dates to Hemingway's youth as "Grace [his mother]. . . made much of hair" and "thought highly of blond hair," like the kind that the young Ernest possessed (Dearborn 2017, 23–24). Hearing at an early age from an authoritative voice that kind of fixation on one's hair and ascribing a value to its color certainly could influence a person going forward. As Hemingway's sister Marcelline recounted, not only did their mother dress them alike but they "wore [their] hair exactly alike" (quoted in Dearborn 2017, 482), "Ernest did not get his first haircut until he was six," and he perhaps "internalized Grace's intense interest until it grew to be a private obsession, entangled with issues of gender, sexual identity, and sexuality" (482). Just as Hemingway's mother's decision to dress him and his sister as twins in girls' clothing[13] might have led to some of the more transgressive aspects of Hemingway's conception of sexuality, so, too, might this early emphasis his mother placed on hair and its beauty have led to its fetishization.

Whatever the initial source for this fixation, as one looks through Hemingway's biography, one can find ample evidence that it was a true part of Hemingway's psychological makeup. Agnes von Kurowsky, the nurse with whom Hemingway fell in love soon after he arrived at the hospital in Milan following his wounding and who would serve as the model for Catherine Barkley in *A Farewell to Arms*, "noted in her diary [in 1918] an incident involving one of her hairpins" (Eby 1998, 60). Eby also notes that "Hadley almost immediately recognized the importance of her reddish auburn hair in first attracting Ernest" (1998, 35), as she wrote in a 1921 letter to her husband, "My hair is turning a nice shade of red it never looked before. I love to have you love my hair. I love yours. Love to pet it back from your forehead" (quoted in Griffin, 1985, 188). Though the references are subtle, one cannot ignore how Jake Barnes initially describes Brett Ashley in *The Sun Also Rises*, the novel emerging from the time of his marriage to Hadley, and is quick to note how "her hair was brushed back like a boy's" and that "she started all that" (*Sun Also Rises & Other Writings*, 2020, 388).

This fascination with hair continued into his marriage to Pauline Pfeiffer. While she "lacked [the] beautiful hair color" Hadley possessed, "Pauline, however, quickly learned how to make her hair exciting" through "boyish cuts not so unlike Ernest's." Then "in July 1929 Pauline dyed her hair blonde as a birthday surprise for Ernest and throughout the 1930s she continued to change her hair color and style frequently" (Eby 1998, 36). Mary Dearborn describes how "in 1933, [Hemingway] was deeply in love with his wife [and] . . . they were having a sort of second honeymoon centered around his persistent sexual fetish, hair" (2017, 328). This phase began when "Ernest bleached or died his," and then "Pauline became a blonde" (328). This clearly affected Hemingway, as he told friends, "Pauline is wonderful," because "she dyed her hair for him" (329). Pauline would perhaps use her husband's fascination with blond hair as a way of keeping him faithful. During his time on Bimini, the Hemingways met Eva Blixen-Finecke, and "a rumor" quickly emerged "that Ernest slept with Eva, who was known as a bit of an adventuress" and "a beautiful blonde" (347), but his wife "was [once again] a blonde . . . and this summer she had her husband transfixed by changing her hair's hue to ash blond" (347). Knowing Hemingway's fixation on hair, Pauline elected to alter hers as a way of commanding her husband's attention away from someone else who might pique his interest.

One of the works written during his marriage to Pauline (and based upon his romance with Agnes von Kurowsky) has sections that reflect Hemingway's interest in hair extended to his writing. In *A Farewell to Arms*, "when [the hospital staff] were all asleep and [Catherine Barkley] was sure they would not call she came in" to Frederic Henry's room, and he was sure to note how he "loved to take her hair down" and that "she had wonderfully beautiful hair" (1995, 114). Later in that same novel, after they have escaped following Frederic's desertion and arrived in Montreaux, they find "a fine coiffeur's place where Catherine went to have her hair done," and while "the woman was waving [Catherine's] hair," Frederic "sat in the little booth and watched. It was exciting to watch and Catherine smiled and talked to [him] and [his] voice was a little thick from being excited" (292). The woman working on Catherine's hair says to Frederic, "Monsieur was very interested. Were you not, monsieur?" (293), perhaps acknowledging this predilection that existed within the author.

Hemingway biographer Kenneth Lynn notes Martha Gellhorn's "beautiful mane of tawny-gold shoulder-length hair" (1995, 464) as part of what caught Hemingway's eye: "Her hair was honey blond then, cut shoulder length, and she had a way of tossing it when she talked" (G. Hemingway 1976, 41). However, there does not seem to be the same degree of play regarding hair as there was with both Hadley and Pauline and would be with his fourth wife, Mary. The novel Hemingway wrote during his courtship of Martha Gellhorn, *For Whom the Bell Tolls*, features some of that intrigue regarding hair with the description of Maria's, which "was the golden brown of a grain field that has been burned dark in the sun . . . cut short all over her head so that it was but a little longer than the fur on a beaver pelt" (1995, 22). Hemingway writes of how his protagonist Robert Jordan "ran his hand over the top of her head" which "he had been wanting to do" and "felt his throat swelling" (67). Pilar, looking at Robert

Jordan and Maria, says, "You could be brother and sister by the look" (67), which seemingly connects to another myth surrounding Hemingway proven true.[14] Jordan's attraction to Maria seems derived in part from her hair, as he says, "It is lovely to feel and I love it very much and it is beautiful and it flattens and rises like a wheatfield in the wind when I pass my hand over it" (*For Whom the Bell Tolls*, 1995, 345). Though this might be a case of "Hemingway spill[ing] far too much ink" indulging this fetish (Dearborn 2017, 400), it does stand as evidence of the importance of this concern in Hemingway's mind and its continued presence even into the years with Gellhorn. In one act that was in keeping with Hemingway's fascination with the cutting of hair, "Martha cut her hair to resemble the fictional Maria and sought Hemingway's approval" (Meyers 1985, 435), but "one suspects, however, that the change may have been Ernest's idea. Not Martha's" (Eby, 1998, 37).

We have perhaps the greatest trove of information about this aspect of Hemingway's psychology in his relationship with his final wife, Mary. Dearborn even makes it clear this was something unique and particular, writing that "Mary's hair was to become a total obsession with Ernest, possibly made more florid and pervasive" because of the assorted head traumas he'd suffered (2017, 466). We see the degree to which Ernest exhibited control over Mary's hair in a 1948 letter to her with instructions regarding how Mary was to have it cut. Hemingway wrote, "Tell him you have decided . . . to wear your hair sleek and long instead of short and curly. But you are keeping the same style of hair-cut. You don't want to lose any of the length and you want the very front, that was so short, to grow into the sweep of the back. You would like the bottom of the hair neatened; trimmed in the same style as it is" (quoted in Eby 1998, 245). In her memoir, Mary recounts how a friend "recommended a hairdresser in Havana and Ernest suggested that I might have my hair bleached, as a present to him"; she "submitted to the bleaching, and Ernest was entranced by the result" (M. Hemingway 1976, 170).

Carl Eby, current president of the Hemingway Society, in his book *Hemingway's Fetishism: Psychoanalysis and the Mirror of Manhood*, describes Hemingway's desire that his wife Mary dye her hair blond: "Hemingway wasn't devoted simply to blonde hair. It could be blonde, red, raven black; it could be long or short. But it was *always* fetishized" (1998, 33). It was not a particular kind of hair that appealed to or attracted Hemingway but hair in general, in its totality.

This fetishization went beyond how his partners wore their hair but also extended to his own. Hemingway writes, in a letter to Harvey Breit (a poet and critic), "Have my head shaved because that is how my fiancée [Mary] likes it. She likes to feel all the holes in my head and the welts. It is sort of fun too. I never know about it before. I thought they were a kind of disgrace. But not here" (*Selected Letters*, 2003, 827) in Kenya.

Verdict: True.

Did Hemingway Hunt for German U-Boats in the Caribbean?

Thomas Bevilacqua

With the United States' entry into World War II following the attack on Pearl Harbor, a concern arose on the home front about any potential encroachment and attack by Axis powers into Allied space, particularly in the oceans that surround the country. There are stories of German U-boats appearing off the coast of New Jersey as well as in the waters near Virginia and North Carolina. It was in that kind of an air that Ernest Hemingway, on his boat the *Pilar* in December 1942 off the northwest coast of Cuba, allegedly came across one of those German vessels.

In his book *Writer, Sailor, Soldier, Spy*, Nicholas Reynolds finds, in materials in both the collection at the JFK Library and biographer Carlos Baker's papers at Princeton, records of the time Hemingway saw "a gray painted vessel . . . that made his pulse quicken" and, upon seeing it in closer detail, said, "[U]nfortunately she is a submarine and pass the word for everyone to be ready to close" (2017, 132–33). Though eventually that German submarine "changed course and sped up . . . moving too fast [and] slipped from sight" (132), the encounter was something for which Hemingway hoped. Reynolds describes how "Hemingway now proposed to fight his war at sea on *Pilar* . . . ready to become what he would call 'a secret agent of my government' . . . the only American sailing in Cuban waters on secret orders" (135). From Cuba, Hemingway would take out his personal fishing boat and keep an eye out for any German naval crafts that found their way into the waters close to America.

Paul Hendrickson notes how "[f]or approximately fourteen months in the wartime forties . . . *Pilar* got converted by her master into a patrol boat, armed with light machine guns, hand grenades, bazookas, and satchel charges of explosives" (2011, 323). Gloria Hemingway described how "in the summer of 1943 . . . the Pilar was armed to the teeth. Two men were stationed in the bow with submachine guns and two in the stern with BARs and hand grenades [while] Papa steered on the flying bridge and up there with him was 'The Bomb,' a huge explosive device, shaped like a coffin, with handles on each end" (1976, 70).

Hemingway's logic was that they could take advantage of the fact that all "the Germans would see . . . a fishing boat going about its business" (Reynolds 2017, 136), but then the "*Pilar* and her crew might be able to lure a Nazi boat to the surface and get in the first blasts before escaping" (Hendrickson 2011, 323). It certainly fits with the popular conception of Hemingway, a kind of cowboy out on the Caribbean waters, but it certainly seems too good to be true. Yet the evidence is there that this was something Hemingway did. This was not just a bit of vigilantism, not an alcohol- or machismo-fueled endeavor, as it was "authorized by the new American ambassador to Cuba, Spruille Braden" (Hendrickson 2011, 323). Though, in his own words, Braden grasped that Hemingway's plan "was against all regulations," Hemingway had been so helpful for his work with the Crook Factory that Braden would "underwrite the new initiative" (Reynolds 2017, 141).

However, save for that encounter with the U-boat Nicholas Reynolds mentions, the *Pilar* "never encountered an enemy ship" (Hendrickson 2011, 324). However, while stuck on the small island of Cayo Confites, Gloria Hemingway recounted seeing a submarine surface. But as Ernest noted, "It's heading AWAY from us"; they were thus unable to use the weaponry housed on the *Pilar* (1976, 88). Though the author was prepared for action, he never was put in a situation where he had to contend with a German craft. Martha Gellhorn was less than convinced of the motivations behind her husband's plan. Allegedly, she believed Hemingway's makeshift U-boat patrols were just a way to get around fuel rationing so that he could go out and drink with his friends.

Hemingway's patrols of the Caribbean waters would make their way into his fiction, specifically the posthumously published novel *Islands in the Stream*. The novel, however, in which protagonist Thomas Hudson goes out into Cuban waters in search of sunken German submarines, climaxes with a shootout.

Verdict: True.

Did Hemingway Examine
F. Scott Fitzgerald's Penis?

Thomas Bevilacqua

Hemingway's tumultuous friendship with F. Scott Fitzgerald has yielded many notorious stories, with one involving Fitzgerald questioning his (quite literal) manhood and Hemingway's instilling confidence back in *The Great Gatsby* author by inspecting him and telling him he had nothing to worry about. This is a story that makes Zelda Fitzgerald's belief (an admittedly incorrect one) that her husband and Hemingway were in love a bit more plausible.[15] But this story of the Hemingway-Fitzgerald friendship does appear to be true.

We gain the clearest window into this moment through Hemingway himself. In *A Moveable Feast*, in the vignette (perhaps somewhat cruelly) titled "A Matter of Measurements," Hemingway describes an encounter when Fitzgerald tells Hemingway, "Zelda said the way I was built could never make any woman happy. . . . She said it was a matter of measurements. I have never felt the same since she said that and I have to know truly" (2009, 162).

The biographical record on Fitzgerald confirms that these were concerns he possessed. David S. Brown describes how these worries might have been on Fitzgerald's mind, writing, "Insecurity might have factored into the reticence that some women detected in Scott" (2017, 267). Also with regard to that aspect of his anatomy, Brown states, "Buttitta [the owner of small bookstore in Asheville's George Vanderbilt Hotel when Fitzgerald spent time in the North Carolina city] . . . recalled a similar conversation" with the author (267). These concerns stayed with Fitzgerald throughout his life, as noted by his biographers, and thus the notion that he would turn to his friend and confidant Hemingway to help assuage his anxiety makes sense.

In the anecdote Hemingway recounts in *A Moveable Feast*, he describes how he told Fitzgerald, "Come out to the office," or the restroom, at which time Fitzgerald showed Hemingway his penis, after which Hemingway told Fitzgerald, "You're perfectly fine. . . . There's nothing wrong with you" (2009, 162). Jeffrey Meyers does note "Hemingway's emphasis on the weak, girlish, feminine aspects of Scott's character" in the memoir that "subtly yet cruelly confirms Zelda's accusations of sexual inadequacy" (1985, 278), which leads one to believe Hemingway's response to Fitzgerald was more about reassuring his friend (at that time).

There has been some pushback from biographers as to whether the incident occurred. Kenneth Lynn's biography of Hemingway notes how this moment "is accepted without question by a number of authorities on Fitzgerald and Hemingway" as it "fits the long-term pattern of self doubt in Fitzgerald as well as his hero worship of Hemingway" (1995, 283), but Lynn finds that "the scene in the men's room . . . bear[s] the hallmark of fantasy" (284). Scott Donaldson notes that "the story sounds like a fabrication as well," especially given that "Hemingway told it in various versions in various places," but "Edmund Wilson's diary of 1932 confirmed that Scott was worried about sexual inadequacy . . . and John Pearl Bishop contributed the information that on at least one occasion Fitzgerald confessed his doubts about the size of his penis to a female dinner partner" (1999, 160). One can also conceive of Hemingway using this story, telling it to burnish his own masculine image, as though he was always the true expert when it came to matters of masculinity and who was a "true man."

Brewster Chamberlin, describing the way that Hemingway writes about Fitzgerald in *A Moveable Feast*, identifies Hemingway's "contempt for what he sees in Fitzgerald as a system of weakness" as well as "his own attraction to Fitzgerald's obvious physical charms when young and beautiful" (2015, 65) as factors creating this pointed portrayal of Fitzgerald, even after he had died. One can see, through this lens, how a story of this nature would fit into Hemingway's desire to portray Fitzgerald in this way that belittled him.

Verdict: Possible.

Did Hemingway Fight
Actor-Director Orson Welles?

Thomas Bevilacqua

As famous as Hemingway's distinctive prose and its effect on American literature were, he's also known for his desire to fight and tendency toward physical violence. Whether in the boxing ring with titans of the sport[16] or with other writers who dared to offend him in some way,[17] the author was not afraid to use his fists when written barbs did not suffice. One of the people with whom Hemingway got into a dustup was the actor and director Orson Welles, though it would not prevent the two from being friendly in the years that followed.

In an interview for the BBC, Welles described Hemingway as a friend while noting that he was not "part of [Hemingway's] clan" because of his willingness to poke fun at the author. In an interview done with director Peter Bogdanovich, Welles said that he "had visitor's cards to some of Ernest's clubs" even though he was "not much of a joiner" when it came to cliques and circles within Hollywood and elsewhere (1998, 27–28). That said, in another interview with Bogdanovich, Welles was sure to note that he was "very fond of Hemingway" (1998, 292), making it clear he held the writer in great esteem.

But before the relationship between Hemingway and Welles reached this amicable period, the two men were sparring partners. The point at which their two lives first intersected was around the Spanish Civil War. Welles recorded narration for *The Spanish Earth*, a 1937 documentary written by Hemingway and John Dos Passos designed to elicit support for the Republicans fighting against the assault of Franco's Nationalists. However, "the Orson Welles version [was] deemed too theatrical" (Chamberlin 2015, 189) and Hemingway himself recorded narration for the film. In his biography of Welles, David Thomson describes how Hemingway "claimed that he had no desire to read [the film's narration] himself—until he heard Welles's voice" as there was a "rising bogusness" (1997, 58) perceived by some, which pushed the author to read his own script for the film aloud.

The fight between Welles and Hemingway, per Welles's recollection, took place in a darkened movie theater while images from the documentary, depicting the horrors of the Spanish Civil War, were projected onto the movie screen. The two men hurled barbs and insults at one another, with Welles and Hemingway lobbing some masculinity-challenging insults at one another until, as Welles described it in the BBC interview, "this great big figure stood up and swung at me. So I swung at him." But then, Welles continued, "The lights came up, we looked at each other, we burst into laughter and became great friends," and "the two of them shar[ed] a bottle of whiskey" afterward (Vaill 2015, 207). It was a story "that Welles enjoyed embroidering as he retold it over many years" (Spaltro 2019). Yet the kernel of truth was there, despite Welles's theatrical embellishments.

From this moment of conflict, a kind of friendship would emerge, one that would even survive Welles being "miffed" that his version of *The Spanish Earth* narration was not going to be used, "especially since he had waived his right to a fee" (Lynn 1995, 451). Welles even mounted multiple radio productions of *A Farewell to Arms*, including one costarring Katharine Hepburn and another with Ginger Rogers. Matthew Asprey Gear writes in a 2020 article for the *Hemingway Review* that Welles "develop[ed] at least three distinct film projects that sought to engage creatively with Ernest Hemingway and his legacy," though none would be fully developed while Welles was still alive (53). Though their interactions started out in this confrontational manner, as time passed, a friendship developed that clearly affected Welles.

Verdict: True.

Was Hemingway Anti-Semitic?

Thomas Bevilacqua

A way of thinking that has poisoned the minds of many is anti-Semitism. Many otherwise great figures and thinkers have displayed this. Unfortunately, Hemingway, much like his friend Ezra Pound and contemporary T. S. Eliot, was one who harbored anti-Semitic views, which appeared both in print and in his personal interactions. The most concrete evidence for Hemingway's anti-Semitic tendencies came early in his career as a writer. The novel that launched Hemingway into the upper stratosphere of American literary celebrity, *The Sun Also Rises*, features a character that would charitably be described as unfortunately depicted and might, if judged uncharitably, be seen as anti-Semitic.

The novel opens with Hemingway introducing the characters of Jake Barnes and Robert Cohn. In the first chapter, there are repeated notings of Cohn's Jewish heritage and obvious references to Jewish stereotypes. Jake Barnes opines how Cohn "got his [nose] most permanently flattened" while boxing, which "certainly improved [it]" (*Sun Also Rises & Other Writings* 2020, 373). Jake also refers to Cohn's "hard, Jewish, stubborn streak" (379). Hemingway portrays Cohn with obvious antipathy that shines through in the prose, alongside constant references to Cohn's status as a Jewish man. It is as though Hemingway says there is this figure (Cohn) who stands for all these things he does not value and he happens to be Jewish, too, as though the two things are somehow linked.

Sadly, Hemingway's tendency toward thoughts that could be understood as anti-Semitic was not limited to how he depicted Jewish characters in his writing. Perhaps nowhere was this more notable than in Hemingway's interactions with the person who served as the basis for the Robert Cohn character—Harold Loeb. Lesley Blume depicts the deterioration of the friendship between Hemingway and Loeb in *Everybody Behaves Badly: The True Story behind Hemingway's Masterpiece* The Sun Also Rises, one that happened under the guise of countless anti-Semitic comments. Blume describes how Loeb "had many powerful advantages that Hemingway lacked—an Ivy League education, seemingly unlimited resources—and the inequity soon created tension between the men" with "one particularly intolerable advantage: [Loeb] was about to publish his first novel, *Doodab*, with Boni & Liveright, a major American publisher" (2016, 56). Though Loeb began to feel something like "blind adoration" for Hemingway and "the more he saw of [Hemingway], the more he liked him" (57), Loeb's acceptance for publication would precipitate the rapid deterioration of their relationship. While in Pamplona and "spoiling for a fight after a week of pent-up tension . . . Hemingway accused [Loeb] of ruining their party" leading to "Loeb . . . ask[ing] Hemingway to step outside" (Blume 2016, 108). Though they did not fight one another that evening, it was clear even in the sober light of the next day that "nothing—not even a sincere apology—could undo what had been done and said." In addition, Loeb "and Hemingway would go their separate ways [but] he couldn't have guessed that Hemingway would soon do something that would link them for the rest of their lives and beyond" (109). But what seemed to prompt Hemingway's feelings toward Loeb was Loeb's Jewish identity. This was something even Hadley identified; she said that "the only thing Ernest had against Harold was that he was Jewish," as "Ernest was very much against Jews" (quoted in Diliberto 2011, 194).

Peter Hays describes how "Loeb felt betrayed and that Hemingway had revealed an anti-Semitic streak" (Hays 2011, 5) through his fictional depiction of Loeb as Robert Cohn in *The Sun Also Rises*, saying that "the book hit [him] like an uppercut" (quoted in Blume 2016, 205). Hemingway made his fictional characters quite close to their real-world inspirations, perhaps for "ritual humiliation," while turning Loeb into a "gross distortion" (205) in the form of Cohn, drawing particularly on anti-Semitic terms and imagery to make those distortions. It is something that stayed with Loeb throughout his entire life. Valerie Hemingway recounted how "quite accidentally [she] met Harold Loeb" and that even "thirty-five years after the novel was published, Loeb was still hurt and puzzled at how he could have inspired such mean-spiritedness in his friend Ernest"; all her conversations with Loeb "inevitably returned to one piteous question: 'Why did Ernest do this to me?'" (V. Hemingway 2005, 213). Loeb wrote a memoir of that time, documenting his relationship and falling out with Hemingway, titled *The Way It Was*.

Hemingway's depiction of Cohn and his treatment of Loeb provide us with the greatest example of Hemingway's anti-Semitism, but these tendencies appear throughout the biographical record on the author as if to say that the most notable example was not a fluke. In one such instance, Michael Reynolds says that "maybe it was the Jewishness" of Lewis Galantière, another American expatriate writer in Paris during the 1920s, "that irritated Hemingway," and "he knew the reference would tickle Ezra [Pound]'s growing anti-Semitism" (*Paris Years*, 1999, 185). After his divorce from Martha Gellhorn, Hemingway wrote to his publisher, Charles Scribner, saying "unpleasant" things about his ex-wife and that "the reason she was never pregnant by him was that he did not care to father half-Jewish children" (Reynolds, *Final Years*, 1999, 208).

In understanding important figures and writers as being humans and not myths, we must acknowledge and accept the aspects of their lives in which their imperfections (and even behavior meriting condemnation) appear.

Verdict: True.

Was Hemingway's Death Accidental?

Thomas Bevilacqua

The news of Hemingway's death shocked the American public when it occurred in 1961. The combination of Hemingway's celebrity (the publication of *The Old Man and the Sea* along with his receiving the Nobel Prize in Literature brought him firmly back into the public eye) and the way in which his physical and mental decline in the final years of his life was kept hidden meant that his death (and, as the details became known, the nature of it) came as quite the surprise.

When these kinds of things occur, events that seem to come out of nowhere or do not seem to make any sense, we will struggle to create a narrative that does make sense. Regarding Hemingway's death, this took the form of a narrative about Hemingway's death being accidental and not a suicide. However, that was not the case, and Hemingway's death must be understood as a suicidal act.

Part of the reason for this alternative narrative comes from how Hemingway's death was initially covered in the press after the fatal shot occurred on July 2, 1961, in Ketchum, Idaho. The *New York Times* report on Hemingway's death stated, "His wife, Mary, said that he had killed himself accidentally while cleaning the weapon." This reporting, perhaps coupled with a desire for it not to be the case that Hemingway took his own life, led to the perception that Hemingway's death was not truly by his own hand. In her autobiography, Mary Welsh Hemingway wrote, "Not consciously lying, I told the press that the shooting had been accidental. It was months before I could face the reality" (1976, 503). Ernest's death so shocked Mary that, in her haze, she told the inquiring press that it had been an accident. "Many of the townspeople and Ernest's friends downplayed the suicide angle," Timothy Christian notes, "in the interviews they gave to reporters," including Chuck Atkinson, a motel owner in Ketchum at that time, saying, "Mary felt it was accidental, and I hope that's the way it will go out," while "Sheriff Frank Hewitt told the press after his preliminary investigation, 'the death looks like an accident'" (Christian 2022, 298). Christian's biography of Mary notes how much of the initial reporting regarding Hemingway's death proffered this narrative of the death being an accident and tells the story of how the *Seattle Post-Intelligencer* reporter Emmett Watson learned that Hemingway's death was a suicide and, for perhaps the first time, revealed that Sheriff Hewitt was the reporter's source that confirmed that Hemingway's death had to be a suicide (Christian 2022, 304–5). This is quite interesting to note, as Hewitt told the press so closely after the event that he had thought it was indeed accidental. People's unwillingness to refer to the real cause of death speaks to the stigma regarding issues of mental health (and anything, like a suicide, that would invite discussion of those issues).

Rather than confronting the possibility of suicide and the difficult questions that might come with it, that Hemingway's death was hastened by his own mental ailments as well as the myriad traumas to which he'd been subject in his life, the inclination was to push things away and keep them hidden and unconsidered. Particularly in a more provincial, small-town environment like Ketchum, there would be an intense desire to avoid the invocation of suicide. Hemingway's prior attempts at taking his own life as well as his conversations about suicide make it clear that it was not foreign to his way of thinking.[18]

The nature of Hemingway's death would remain unclear until the 1966 publication of A.E. Hotchner's *Papa Hemingway*. Hotchner made a definitive claim surrounding the nature of Hemingway's death, that it was a suicide and not an accident. Hotchner, a good friend of Hemingway's during the final years of the author's life, starts the foreword to his book by stating that on July 2, 1961, Hemingway "put a shotgun to his head and killed himself" (1966, xi), making a clear claim that went against the prevailing narrative. Hotchner also wrote, after hearing Mary's initial allegation of Hemingway's death being accidental, "I could not fault Mary for covering up. She was not prepared to accept what had happened and that's what came out when she had to explain" (334–35). Mary sued the publishers in an attempt to stop the book from being released, but Mary lost her lawsuit, and the notion that Hemingway's death happened by accident was dispelled.

Verdict: False.

Did Hemingway Play the Cello?

Thomas Bevilacqua

We think of Hemingway as a figure of diverse interests—big-game hunter, fisherman, war-covering journalist, and on and on that list goes. Yet one way of seeing Hemingway that does not leap immediately into people's minds is as a musician. There is a great lineage of authors profoundly influenced by their relationship with music, as either performers or listeners. There is, for example, the jazz-inflected writing of Jack Kerouac and Langston Hughes. But Hemingway grew up playing the cello as part of a musically inclined home, thanks to the work of his mother, Grace Hall Hemingway.

Michael Reynolds notes Hemingway's familiarity with the musical world. "As a boy, Hemingway was no stranger to classical music," Reynolds notes. "Grace took Ernest to Chicago opera during his early years, and the Chicago Symphony played an annual benefit series in Oak Park, where a high percentage of the middle-class gentry were not only musically conversant but actually skilled musicians" (*Young Hemingway*, 1999, 150). Grace was clearly the reason for any of Hemingway's exposure to the world of music.

In her youth, Grace "had an excellent voice" and even "began to think as an adolescent of a serious singing career" (Dearborn 2017, 15). Bernice Kert notes how Grace was encouraged to receive "more voice lessons and [attend] a program of foreign language study in preparation for the operatic theater" after her 1891 graduation from high school (1998, 24). Grace went to New York and studied under Madame Louisa Cappianni, who, "believ[ing] that Grace possessed a remarkable voice . . . arranged an audition for her pupil with the authorities at the Metropolitan Opera and there was the possibility of a contract for Grace" (Kert 1998, 25). However, because of the "pleading" (25) letters of Clarence Hemingway with offers of marriage, Grace withdrew from this path and course of study after "a concert in Madison Square Garden" to cover her instruction, a concert for which "the press notices were good, but the experience of performing behind glaring footlights was hard on her weak eyes" (25). Grace would ultimately marry Clarence (a.k.a. Ed) on October 1, 1896, ending any notions she might have had of a professional singing career, though she supplemented her husband's income by offering voice and piano lessons.

While her decision to marry Ed and start a family took her away from a career as a professional musician, it did not stop her from making music a central concern in her home. When Grace led the construction of a new home for the Hemingways in Oak Park, she made sure it was "her dream house" with "a music studio where she could teach and organize recitals" (Kert 1998, 30). The construction of this home, representing Grace's desire to "move upward" as "she sought cultural and intellectual fulfillment" created in Ernest a "resentment of Grace [that] hardened in his adult life" for "the selfishness of her decision" (Kert 1998, 31) to take the Hemingways out of the home they'd known and move them into this new one.

Perhaps because a potential professional music career was stifled due to the demands of marriage and family, Grace directed her children toward that world. The Hemingway matriarch "saw her responsibility as primarily artistic—to exhort and inspire and open the souls of her children to the noble world of creativity" (Kert 1998, 35). In her memoir *At the Hemingways*, Ernest's sister Marcelline recounts how "at home we had a family orchestra: father on his cornet . . . Ernie with his cello, I with my violin and Mother at the piano. Sunny also played the piano and Uncle Tyley had his flute" (Sanford 1999, 123). Marcelline writes of how "Ernest worked hard on his cello, but had great difficulty in tuning his strings and playing in key[;] . . . though he wanted very much to be a good cellist, he was finding many other interests" and "disliked the long hours of practicing the cello after school and longed to be with his friends [and] . . . gave it up by his senior year" (123). Marcelline paints a picture of the Hemingways as something like the Carter family or the von Trapps: a household that doubled as a musical group. Grace certainly encouraged this, with "as many as three hundred guests eventually crowded into the music room and on the balcony for her recitals [and] she scheduled lessons and returned to musical composition," even "calling her family to supper" by "sing[ing] out the summons" (Kert 1998, 34).

However, Ernest and his brother Leicester "were ambivalent about their mother's musical activities [and] did not like to hear her even suggest that she had given up operatic stardom for marriage and motherhood" (Kert 1998, 34), which might have led to Hemingway's apathy toward becoming a proficient musician in his youth, something he would address in an interview later in his life, which was published in the spring 1958 edition of *Paris Review*. Hemingway tells interviewer George Plimpton how he "used to play cello," as his mother "thought [he] had ability, but [he] was absolutely without talent," even saying, "That cello—I played it worse than anyone on earth" (Hemingway 2006, 47). One can also infer the resentment Hemingway felt toward his mother when he said, in that same interview, that she "kept [him] out of school a whole year to study music and counterpoint" which kept him from going "out [and] doing other things" that he was ostensibly more interested in (47).

Hemingway's interest in music lasted long after he gave up the cello. In a November 28, 1918, letter to his family, a letter collected in volume 1 of *The Letters of Ernest Hemingway*, he makes sure to note the numerous operas he's seen while in Italy: "I go to the opera though at the Scala. Have seen Aida, Ghismonda, Mose, Barbiere Di Seville and Mephistophele with Toscanini conducting. Going to see D'Annunzio's La Nave soon. Wish they'd give Carmen or La Boheme or something interesting. I know lots of singers who hang around the American Bar" (2011, 160).

Hilary Justice, in an article for *The Hemingway Review*, documents the voluminous record collection Hemingway had at the Finca Vigía: "Certain of the bins in the built-in (probably custom) speaker cabinet are located higher than Hemingway's fourth wife, Mary, could easily have reached; these may contain albums that Ernest Hemingway preferred. In these higher bins, albums with worn jackets suggesting frequent play contain works of Romantic, Classical, and especially Baroque composers. Their composition styles and formal achievements may have provided the soundtrack for Hemingway's writing in the 1940s and '50s" (2005, 98). Justice also notes, "Perhaps surprisingly, Hemingway's single most important musical artifact is the Finca Vigía house itself. Its open floor plan, high ceilings, and tiled floor reflect an architectural pragmatism appropriate to the tropical climate, but also coincidentally render the house almost acoustically perfect," which allowed for the home to function "as a house-sized stereo system" (97).

Verdict: True.

Did Hemingway's Third Child, Gloria (Born Gregory), Transition and Receive Gender Confirmation Surgery?

Thomas Bevilacqua

When one is the child of a major figure in the culture, life can be deeply challenging. It poses a challenge to just try to make one's way in the world when a parent casts an enormous shadow. But it's an even greater challenge when the parent is known for an over-the-top masculinity while the child struggles with identity and sexuality. And that's what Ernest and Pauline's youngest child, Gloria (born Gregory), had to confront. As Gloria's son John says in his memoir *Strange Tribe*, "I couldn't help but pick up on the obsession my dad had with his father. He never wore it on his sleeve, but the conflict between the two, and with his own sexuality, was ever-present" (J. Hemingway 2007, 15). By age twelve, Gloria was cross-dressing, frequently wearing her stepmother's stockings. In 1995, at age sixty-four, Gloria received gender confirmation surgery and began to live with Gloria as her preferred name.

In her book on the marriage between Hemingway and Pauline Pfeiffer, Ruth Hawkins records how in 1933, Pauline "went off to Africa with Ernest for eight months, leaving [their two-year-old-child] alone with Ada [Stern, the nanny for the Hemingways]," and the separation traumatized Gregory.[19] Ada "governed by fear, threatening to leave him just like his parents did if he misbehaved." For comfort, the child "retrieved his mother's silk stockings from her chest of drawers to feel close to her," thus "beginning the habit of resorting to women's clothing whenever facing stressful situations" (2012, 270). Gloria, in a piece for 1989 *Fame* magazine titled "The Sons Also Rise," recounted one time in which Ernest found her wearing a pair of those stockings and seeing in Ernest's face "such devastation and horror" that it seemed to say, "What's wrong with the family? My God! Is he doing this too?" (quoted in J. Hemingway 2007, 45). Valerie Hemingway, who was married to Gloria for over twenty years, describes how "whenever he was under stress, he put on a pair of nylon stockings, and it acted like a tranquilizer to soothe his nerves or allay his fears. It gave him comfort and strength" (V. Hemingway 2005, 236). Gloria told Valerie this after explaining how as a child she felt abandoned and unloved by her mother and "He associated stockings only with his mother, who was gone" (237).

In *Strange Tribe*, John Hemingway recalled the first time he saw his father dressed in women's clothing. John writes, "Even if his entrance wasn't staged, on a subconscious level, it seemed in part to be a reenactment of the morning when Ernest had walked in on him as a boy." He "looked surprised . . . his cherry-red lipstick was smudged, and he reminded [John] of a four-year-old who's decided to play with his mother's cosmetics" (2007, 51). This seems to suggest the psychic centrality of this moment when Gloria was discovered by her father who "was just too masculine to believe" (quoted in J. Hemingway 2007, 45), as Gloria put it in that *Fame* magazine piece. It was a moment Gloria returned to and reenacted. For, as John put it, "if he'd really wanted to keep it a secret, there were a number of places where he could have changed before coming home" (2007, 51).

Gloria was also profoundly affected by her mother's death and the events leading up to it. Gloria wrote in her 1976 memoir that "in 1951 . . . I got into some trouble on the West Coast for taking a mind-stimulating drug before such things had become fashionable" (G. Hemingway 1976, 6). However, while Gloria, in 1976, wanted to present this incident as related to intoxication, in reality, "Greg had been arrested in the women's bathroom of a Los Angeles movie theater," which led to "an acrimonious shouting match over the phone" between Ernest and Pauline, who had come to Los Angeles to post the bail money (Dearborn 2017, 544). Gloria recounts hearing of the phone call through her aunt Jinny, "who hated [her] father's guts," and describes how "the conversation started out calmly enough. But soon enough [Pauline] was shouting into the phone and sobbing uncontrollably" (1976, 6). Ruth Hawkins recalled that Ernest felt that "Pauline bore the blame for all Gregory's problems; if she had been a better mother, and less permissive, none of this would have happened" (2012, 270). After this shouting match that "degenerated into accusations, blame-laying, vituperation, and general misunderstanding," Pauline "woke with stomach pains; within hours she was dead" (Reynolds, *Final Years*, 1999, 242–43), as "Pauline's blood pressure had gone sky high, then dropped to nothing, causing her to die of shock" (Hawkins 2012, 271).

Ernest forged a connection between the arrest (and the predilection for cross-dressing that led to it) and Pauline's death. During a visit to Cuba sometime after those legal troubles, Gloria asked about "'the trouble' . . . on the Coast," hoping that it "really wasn't so bad," to which Ernest replied, "No? Well it killed Mother" (G. Hemingway 1976, 8). Because Ernest had "almost always been right about things" (8), Gloria took these words to be the truth, and thus she "never saw [her] father again" (8). Gloria was already grappling with sexuality, a struggle that ran against conventional, mainstream thinking of that time (and, sadly, is still often similarly misperceived today).

To hear such words from her father—that an event in part connected to her sexual orientation precipitated the death of her mother—would have been devastating.

In 1995, Gloria underwent gender-affirming surgery. In her memoir, Valerie recounts receiving a phone call from "the owner of the Thunderbird Motel" in Missoula, Montana, saying "Greg—or Gloria, as he called himself"—had gone to Trinidad, had "had a sex change operation," but "had not stayed for the postoperative period and now was hemorrhaging badly" (2005, 293). John described how, after hearing the news that his father had received gender-affirming surgery, he and his brother Patrick went and found her at that same Thunderbird Motel "adjusting to his newfound status as a woman . . . wearing female clothes and a wig" and either speaking "in a masculine way" or "as he imagined the female part of him—called 'Gloria'—would speak" (J. Hemingway 2007, 176–77).

Though Gregory underwent that gender-affirming surgery in 1995, she presented as both Gregory and Gloria for the rest of his life. As John wrote, using mostly male pronouns, "Out in the open, he usually dressed as a man, but on occasion, when he felt like expressing himself, he'd hop on a bus in his Gloria mode" (J. Hemingway 2007, 177). In 2001, Gloria "went to a party at a friend's house in the Grove [Coconut Grove, Miami] . . . in a long black evening gown, with black high heels and blond wig" and seeming "in excellent spirit" as she danced and laughed (J. Hemingway 2007, 206). However, leaving the party, she decided to take off the dress and even the "[underwear] had to go," so observers might spot "the elderly, somewhat overweight exhibitionist wandering past" (207). After "the partying and the booze caught up" with her and she slept on the beach, Gloria was found by a police officer, who realized "she'd have to arrest" her and that Gloria "needed help" (207–8). Gloria would eventually be transferred to Miami-Dade County Women's Correctional Facility, where her "heart went into fibrillation on the morning of October 1, 2001, fifty years to the day (almost to the hour)" of her mother's death, and she "died alone, having endured the pain for as long as" she could (J. Hemingway 2007, 212).

Verdict: True.

Did Hemingway Have an Affair with Model and Socialite Jane Mason?

Thomas Bevilacqua

In "The Short Happy Life of Francis Macomber," Hemingway describes Margot Macomber as "an extremely handsome and well-kept woman of the beauty and social position which had, five years before, commanded five thousand dollars as the price of endorsing, with photographs, a beauty product which she had never used" (*The Short Stories* 2003, 4). The inspiration for this character, as well as for Helen Bradley in *To Have and Have Not*, was Jane Mason. Per Brewster Chamberlin's *The Hemingway Log* (2015), Mason, an American socialite married to Pan American Airlines cofounder Grant Mason, met and befriended Ernest and Pauline on September 23, 1931, on the *Île de France*, a voyage that Carlos Baker records as "a merry and drunken crossing" (1969, 222).

This first meeting while crossing the Atlantic Ocean led to a close and powerful bond between the famous author and the beautiful Mason. As Paul Hendrickson notes, "Back in the early thirties, when she was still youthful and blond and high-strung and high-sexed and wed to an old Yale clubman and high executive of Pan American Airways in Cuba," Mason "was Hemingway's wild-assed drinking partner and fishing companion" (2011, 51). During one of these fishing trips, Carlos Baker writes, Jane "chartered a boat in the hope of catching more fish than Ernest did" (1969, 286), displaying a competitive streak that Ernest both shared and more than likely appreciated.

In addition to being a drinking and fishing companion for Ernest, Jane played a much more intimate role in Hemingway's life, as the American socialite was "probably [Hemingway's] lover" and "many

Hemingway chroniclers have assumed it for fact" even though "no one's ever been able to establish this as an indisputable fact" (Hendrickson 2011, 51). We see the documentation of an affair between Hemingway and Mason in Carlos Baker's biography of Hemingway. Baker records an incident from early in their interactions that perhaps hints at the nature of their relationship: "Jane was present for several days' fishing about the *Antina* early in May [1932]," Baker recalls, "and one entry in the log, not in Ernest's hand, read simply, 'Ernest loves Jane'" (1969, 228).

"How [Hemingway and Mason] conducted their love affair is unclear" (Kert 1998, 249), but the evidence points to the two of them taking their relationship beyond the friendly to something more romantic. William Deibler notes that "Cuban writer Enrique Cirules has no doubts" as to whether the affair between Hemingway and Jane Mason transpired, as "in his book *Ernest Hemingway in the Romano Archipelago*, he asserts unequivocally" the veracity of that romantic connection, which "was gossiped about across the island" (Deibler 2014, 61).

Gloria Hemingway recalled in her memoir how "during the late 1930s he used to cuckold Mother unmercifully in Havana with an American lady friend" even claiming that "once he almost broke his toe jumping out of a hotel window when [Pauline] arrived at the place unexpectedly" (G. Hemingway 1976, 92). There was disagreement between the Hemingway children about the veracity of such an affair, as John Hemingway, the author's first son, said that such an affair did "not [occur] on the boat" as "too much was going on, and Papa would not carry on in front of the crew. They were his buddies" (quoted in Kert 1998, 249). Michael Reynolds takes a skeptical view of the affair, writing, "Many would say that a torrid affair took place that summer between Ernest and Jane, but letters, the *Anita* log, and the *Havana Post* show that Hemingway had little time for adultery" (Reynolds, *1930s*, 1999, 131).

A. E. Hotchner's book *Hemingway in Love* features his remembrances of conversations with the author and directly addresses the Jane Mason rumors. As recorded by Hotchner, Hemingway states that Mason "didn't let her marriage . . . get in the way of her adventures with [him]" (2015, 133) and that "unlike hiding [his] affair with Pauline from Hadley, [he] wanted Pauline to know what was going on with Jane" (134). Though Hotchner's book was written long after the actual event (possibly) transpired, it does point more definitively to the fact that there was truly an affair between Hemingway and Mason. Describing Hemingway's references to Jane Mason in his "The Art of the Short Story," Miriam Mandel (coeditor of a volume of Hemingway's letters that show the beginning of his relationship, whatever kind it was, with Mason), sums it up: "His remarks are subjective, filtered through time and memory. The most likely truth is . . . that we shall never know" (2020, 112).

We might look to the actions of both Hemingway and Mason after the alleged affair seemed to have run its course and see in them the jealousy indicative of two former lovers. When Hemingway got wind that Jane and *Esquire* editor Arnold Gingrich had an affair, he responded by saying, "Goddamn editor comes down to Bimini and sees a blonde, and he hasn't been the same since" (quoted in Gingrich 1966, 322), reflecting the jealousy that could emerge when one's paramour elects to take up with another. Gingrich seems to have noticed the similarities between Mason and the character of Helen Bradley in the upcoming *To Have and Have Not* and performed an "intervention on her behalf": "Ernest agreed to tone down the more obvious references" to Mason though he still "painted an unflattering portrait" of Mason through the character of Helen (Hawkins 2012, 192).

There was also jealousy felt by Mason when Hemingway began to have an affair with another woman. Paul Hendrickson recounts a story that describes Jane as having "been furious over Hemingway's love affair with Martha Gellhorn" and reacting by stealing "Carlos [Gutiérrez, then Hemingway's first mate on the *Pilar*] away . . . to be mate on her own boat" (2011, 322). None of these actions by either Hemingway or Mason is definitive proof that the two had an affair, but they all do reflect the kinds of passions and irrational feelings indicative of two who had been involved in that way.

Verdict: Probable.

Did Hemingway Have a Nickname for His Penis?

Thomas Bevilacqua

When we start investigating the lives of famous people, those figures who tower like giants in our collective minds, we discover that so many of them are just like us in all our interesting and unusual ways and, perhaps, even go beyond, into behavior that transcends those normal idiosyncrasies. Hemingway was no exception to this. Some of these things were more quotidian, while others a bit further out there. One of those more "further out there" examples is that Hemingway had a name for his penis: Mr. Scrooby.

Michael Reynolds references a letter Ernest sent to Martha Gellhorn that "closed . . . [by] telling her that Mr. Scrooby (his penis) now referred to himself as 'us'" (*Final Years*, 1999, 30). Caroline Moorehead's biography of Gellhorn references the nickname as well; she writes, "After dinner, when they are alone, there would be 'Mister Scrooby, as friendly as a puppy and as warm as fur'" (2004, 137). Rose Marie Burwell, in her work on the later years of Hemingway's life and his posthumous novels, draws on materials housed at the JFK Library in Boston to confirm that it was "the name he used for his penis" (1996, 208). The Mr. Scrooby nickname appears repeatedly throughout the biographical record of Hemingway's marriage to his fourth wife, Mary. Ernest uses the nickname in a Christmas 1944 letter to Mary, saying that "Mr. Scrooby has risen at this point" (quoted in Fuentes 1984, 373).

Carl Eby discusses a 1947 letter in which "Ernest tells Mary that 'Mr. Scrooby' (Ernest's pet name for his penis) made a 'tent' out of the bed as he was writing, and he was afraid it would 'do an Old Faithful' before she got home. After a slight detour he lapses back into a reverie about Mary's hair and 'up comes Mr. S. again'" (1998, 246).

Dawn Trouard asks in her review for the *Washington Post* of *Hemingway: The Final Years* by Michael Reynolds, "Is there anyone who wants to know that Hemingway's nickname for his penis was Mr. Scrooby?" Whether or not anyone does, as we know that it was.

Verdict: True.

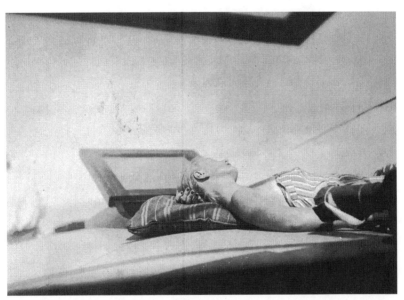

The socialite and model Jane Mason became one of Hemingway's frequent companions in the 1930s to the extent that many believe that Mason and Hemingway had an affair. Mason would also serve as the inspiration for figures in Hemingway's fiction, such as Margot Macomber. Toby and Betty Bruce collection of Ernest Hemingway, Penn State University

Ernest Hemingway's life certainly made good use of his passport, but it also came at great expense. He was involved in numerous accidents and suffered a myriad of injuries and ailments. Later in his life, Hemingway survived multiple plane crashes in Africa that left him with wounds that hastened his physical decline and led to the end of his life. Toby and Betty Bruce collection of Ernest Hemingway, Penn State University

This photograph famously documents the only meeting between Hemingway and the Cuban revolutionary Fidel Castro. The two met at a fishing tournament bearing Hemingway's name, and Castro told the author that his novel For Whom the Bell Tolls was his guerrilla manual. Though the two men did (briefly) meet, they certainly could not be understood as friends. Photofest

The Hemingway-Gellhorn marriage was a tempestuous pairing. After the initial courtship, which brought about the end of his marriage to second wife Pauline, the relationship was tinged with animosity and resentment, which led to an extremely acrimonious end. In turn, this would lead to allegations that Gellhorn was a lesbian, allegations that could not be corroborated. Photofest

One of Ernest Hemingway's favorite possessions was his boat, Pilar. *Hemingway managed to suffer a gunshot wound while fishing on that boat, and he turned it into a makeshift patrol boat ready to attack any German U-boats entering American waters, using his supply of grenades.* Toby and Betty Bruce collection of Ernest Hemingway, Penn State University

Hemingway's life of adventure and action was certainly no myth, but his reputation as a famous quote machine was certainly exaggerated. Many of the quotations attributed to Hemingway were never actually uttered by him. Toby and Betty Bruce collection of Ernest Hemingway, Penn State University

Hemingway's wounding during World War I was one of the informative moments of his life and would lead to many of the myths surrounding him, including that he fought in the conflict and that after his wounding, he carried an Italian soldier to safety. Toby and Betty Bruce collection of Ernest Hemingway, Penn State University

World War II was an eventful time for Hemingway, as he would both meet J. D. Salinger (eventual author of Catcher in the Rye) *and shoot a toilet in the Ritz Hotel in Paris, France. However, his experience during World War II did not extend to the actual battlefield, as the myth that he killed 122 Nazis is false.* Photofest

Given that much of Hemingway's writing focused on wartime experience, one might conclude that Hemingway was one who thought war was a good thing. However, Hemingway's experience during World War I, what he witnessed, gave him an extremely critical view of warfare and a great deal of scorn for those in power who were more than happy to send young men off to senseless deaths. Toby and Betty Bruce collection of Ernest Hemingway, Penn State University

Hemingway's wounds during World War I did not come from being a combatant. Rather, it was participating in the canteen service—delivering coffee, cigarettes, mail, chocolate, and other things to Italian soldiers—that led to Hemingway's injuries on July 8, 1918. Toby and Betty Bruce collection of Ernest Hemingway, Penn State University

Hemingway's love of sports was not limited to fishing. He also enjoyed boxing (taking the time to spar with former heavyweight champion Gene Tunney) and baseball (managing a little league team in Cuba). Toby and Betty Bruce collection of Ernest Hemingway, Penn State University

"Windemere"

"Windemere"

"Windemere"

The Hemingway family's 1919 trip to Windemere, their cottage on Walloon Lake in Michigan, featured a guest, Ruth Arnold. The close relationship between Ruth and Grace Hall Hemingway, Ernest's mother, led to speculation that the two women were in love with each other. Toby and Betty Bruce collection of Ernest Hemingway, Penn State University

Did Hemingway Carry an Italian Soldier to Safety during World War I?

Thomas Bevilacqua

July 8, 1918, was one of the days that changed Ernest Hemingway's life forever, as it served as his initiation into a world of violence and chaos that would be the focus of his writing. At Fossalta di Piave in Northern Italy, Hemingway would be injured by fragments from a mortar shell explosion at the front lines. This event, which left pieces of shell and mortar in Hemingway while rendering him unconscious, provided material for the legend of Hemingway as the ultimate heroic masculine figure.

The story goes that after suffering this injury, Hemingway carried one of the Italian soldiers who was with him at the front lines to safety. This aspect of Hemingway's wartime experience elevates it; Hemingway is not just someone who suffered a wound but rather a heroic figure who performed acts that defy logic and realism, reflecting the notions of courage with which he would later engage in his fiction. However, based on much of the evidence that remains, it is quite likely that things did not happen in this way.

In a July 14, 1918, letter written to Hemingway's parents following his wounding, Ernest's friend Ted Brumback states that "a third Italian was badly wounded" along with him and that Ernest, "after he had regained consciousness, picked [the soldier] up . . . and carried him to the first aid dug-out," though Ernest did not recall the incident by the following day (Hemingway 2011, 1:115). Hemingway described the experience of wounding in a later letter by saying, "My feet felt like I had rubber boots full of water on. Hot water," and adding, "I got up again and got my wounded into the dug out" (1:130), both letters mentioning another person or other people Hemingway took care of amid his own injuries. The *Kansas City Star* reported on the incident, saying that Hemingway carried "several wounded Italian soldiers into a dressing station" (quoted in Florczyk 2014, 77). Even Mary Dearborn's 2017 biography of Hemingway recounts the author "lifting the body of a third, badly wounded soldier"[20] (59) as he made his way to safety.

While this has been somewhat accepted as part of the Hemingway narrative, there is much that casts doubt on its veracity. Steven Florczyk tells of how "Bates [Robert W. Bates, Hemingway's commanding officer] did not say anything about Hemingway aiding another wounded man" and that he "referred to a soldier [who shielded Hemingway] from the explosion instead" (2014, 80). "The final Red Cross report for the period," Steve Paul observes, possessed "no mention of [Hemingway's] carrying a fallen soldier to safety" (2017, 156). The depiction of Hemingway in Carlos Baker's biography of Hemingway reportedly "inflamed Bates" who "was neither the first nor the last to label Hemingway a braggart and liar" (Bates 2009, 58).

Robert Trogdon identifies a potential source for this myth in the writing of Guy Hickok, the Paris bureau chief for the *Brooklyn Daily Eagle* who became a friend of Hemingway during his time in the French capital. Trogdon states that "it is not clear whether it was Hemingway who exaggerated parts of his biography—such as his wounding during World War I—when relating them to Hickok or whether it was Hickok who embellished them for readers." For the most part, the accounts that Hickok wrote do not match those provided by Hemingway's biographers or by his correspondence: "Hickok's reporting could be the source [as] an examination of many of his articles written from Paris indicates that he often focused on outrageous and outlandish happenings" (2014, 183–84). The combination of Hemingway's tendency toward exaggeration coupled with a friendly reporter to pass it along could establish this narrative as the prominent one in people's minds.

Another thing that perhaps solidified the idea that this happened to Hemingway during his own wounding was what transpired in his novel *A Farewell to Arms*, which depicts one man's experience at the front in World War I. When Hemingway describes Frederic Henry's wounding, he writes: "My legs felt warm and wet and my shoes were wet and warm inside" (1995, 55). This scene, with Frederic Henry noting how "there were three others to locate" (55) after his wounding, became what we assumed happened to Hemingway.

Jackson Benson identifies the tendencies in even the most sophisticated and thoughtful readers of Hemingway to see his protagonists strictly "as extensions of their author, essentially 'disguised' personal histories" (1989, 346). This is perhaps one reason why this myth has persisted and become so embedded in readers' perception of Hemingway. They recall Frederic Henry looking for others to save and assume that is what Hemingway did as well. Though Hemingway obviously incorporates elements of his experience into *Farewell*—one can see the similar word choices in how Hemingway described his experience and how Frederic Henry experiences things—Hemingway's creation of this epic story of heroism through the narrative of *Farewell* casts in stone this image of Hemingway as hero for many people. As Benson writes in his article, this kind of approach creates "not only flawed criticism and weak interpretation but a view of the fiction that has been very narrow, since it has been often formulated out of a reaction to what we think we know about a man" (1989, 347).

Verdict: Improbable.

Did Hemingway Work as a Russian Spy?

Thomas Bevilacqua

Hemingway's experiences during the late 1930s and 1940s seem like something pulled from the best works of espionage fiction. Depictions of Hemingway's time spent carrying a makeshift arsenal on the *Pilar* and patrolling the Caribbean for German U-boats, something discussed in this book, in addition to the role he played in the American intelligence apparatus, seem like the work of Alan Furst or Graham Greene. Another story of Hemingway's intersection with the intelligence apparatus, one that stems from his support for the Loyalist cause in the Spanish Civil War (that was supported by the Soviet Union), is that he served as a Russian spy (a storyline seemingly pulled from Furst's novel *Night Soldiers*). However, while Hemingway made connections with certain Soviet officers and figures during his time in Spain, he cannot be understood as having served as a Russian spy.

Hemingway traveled to Spain in 1937 to cover the war for the North American Newspaper Alliance. Though ostensibly there to report, Hemingway also displayed a keen investment in the Republicans (or Loyalists) in their fight against the Franco-led (and Axis supported) Nationalists. Hemingway's serving with this cause, and its proximity to power, might have influenced him. Though "Hemingway's commitment to the Loyalists was not quite as deep-seated as that of others . . . he was earnest in support of the cause" which "brought out many of his best qualities, inspiring him to boost morale and secure aid in whatever form he could, even when it put him in harm's way, as it often did" (Hutchisson 2016, 151).

Antony Beevor notes in his history of the Spanish Civil War that "it is difficult to ascertain how much Hemingway was influenced by the privileged information he received from senior party cadres and Russian advisers. Being taken seriously by experts distorted his vision. It made him prepared to sign moral blank cheques on behalf of the Republic" (2001, 178). This blank check, which overrode his instincts to "not [be] a joiner" and the fact that "his opposition to the juggernaut of fascism was not the same thing as supporting communism" (Hutchisson 2016, 151), might have even extended beyond the Spanish Civil War into World War II.

Nicholas Reynolds, in his book *Writer, Sailor, Soldier, Spy: Ernest Hemingway's Secret Adventures, 1935–1961*, recounts how "in the winter of 1940-41" Hemingway "agreed to work hand in hand with the NKVD [the intelligence agency and secret police of the Soviet Union] in the fight against Fascism, and he met in secret with Soviet spies during World War II" though "he did not intend to be disloyal to his own country" (2017, 212). While in the eyes of some, particularly those whipped up into a frenzy by Joseph McCarthy, there was no distinction that could be made, Hemingway's words and actions make it clear he was not serving as a Russian spy during those times. Rather, he was a member of the broader anti-Fascist intelligence community.

After those contacts in World War II, there was never any engagement between Hemingway and Soviet intelligence. Nicholas Reynolds notes that "if anyone in the NKVD thought about Hemingway after 1950, no one wrote it down" and "there is no evidence that the NKVD contemplated getting back in touch with him ever again or that he ever met another Soviet spy in the flesh" (2017, 220). Had Hemingway truly served as a Soviet spy, as opposed to someone focused on the fight against anti-Fascism, this would likely not have been the case, particularly as the Cold War began and the Soviet Union saw the United States as its great rival.

Verdict: False.

Was Hemingway an Art Collector?

Thomas Bevilacqua

Hemingway had a reverence for the work of visual artists. When discussing his approach to writing, Hemingway alluded to painting as the best way to describe his art. In *A Moveable Feast*, Hemingway writes:

> If I walked down by different streets to the Jardin du Luxembourg in the afternoon I could walk through the gardens and then go to the Musée du Luxembourg where the great paintings were that have now mostly been transferred to the Louvre and the Jeu de Paume. I went there nearly every day for the Cézannes and to see the Manets and the Monets and the other Impressionists that I had first come to know about in the Art Institute at Chicago. I was learning something from the painting of Cézanne that made writing simple true sentences far from enough to make the stories have the dimensions that I was trying to put in them. (2009, 23)

Hemingway's appreciation for art as inspiration for his writing was not limited to art at museums. Throughout his life, Hemingway amassed a modest collection of artworks from those figures he encountered and whose work he enjoyed. Perhaps most famous among them is Joan Miró's piece *The Farm*. Carlos Baker tells how "Evan Shipman [a poet and friend of Hemingway's in the 1920s] had been coveting the picture" but "magnanimously offered to shoot dice [with Hemingway] for the right to buy it," to which Hemingway agreed. And then after "scurr[ying] around borrowing the money" to pay for it, Hemingway "triumphantly brought home the picture" (1969, 158). Hugh Eakin, in a piece for *Vanity Fair*, recounts how "according to Hemingway, the two then decided to shoot dice for it, and he won. (Shipman later said it was a coin toss and that he won but that he let Hemingway have it anyway.)" Hemingway's acquisition of the painting also led to his meeting the Murphys, Gerald and Sara. This would be a momentous crossing of paths, as "no talk of the expatriate 'good life' would be complete without an introduction to the Murphys, members of the American upper class and occasional hosts to Hemingway" who would "monthly or seasonally [visit] their Paris flat for the latest exhibit or costume ball" while "Hemingway would spend many hours in the following summer" with them (Fitch 1983, 201–2).

Amanda Vaill describes how Gerald Murphy "met a young writer who was interested" in that Miró painting though he "confess[ed] that he wanted to buy the picture and couldn't afford it" (1999, 166). Gerald "told him his instinct was right, the painting was wonderful—and Hemingway scraped together the $200 it cost by borrowing from friends and working as a stevedore in the market at Les Halles" (166). Bernice Kert differs slightly in her account, saying that the money Hemingway cobbled together was "mostly from Hadley herself" (1998, 168). But whether the source was his Parisian compatriots or his own wife, Hemingway possessed the painting as "Dos Passos and Shipman and Ernest carried the canvas back to number 113 in a slow-moving Paris taxicab and hung it over the living room couch" with "Hadley appreciat[ing] the uniqueness of such a gift" (Kert 1998, 168).

This notable acquisition by Hemingway went on to have an interesting story of its own into the author's final years and even after his death. In late 1958, Hemingway elected to lend the painting, which by then had hung at Finca Vigía for many years, to the Museum of Modern Art in New York for a major Miró exhibition.

After being delayed by the fall of the Batista regime, the work arrived in New York. But "all those years at the Finca had done ravages. It was a damp, tropical climate, and the Hemingways kept the old house wide open to the outside. There were ceiling leaks. And there was nothing protecting the surface of the painting itself" and thus "Miró's brilliant colors were gone. The surface was covered with grime and mildew, and the paint was cracking. Flecks of whitewash had splattered across the sky; there were water stains and candle-wax residue. And termites had eaten away the back of the painting to the point that in a few places the paint had no canvas underneath" (Eakin 2018). Hemingway agreed that the painting could remain at the museum after the exhibition was over and be subject to a restoration effort, one "nearly as long as it had taken Miró to paint it" (Eakin 2018). The painting would remain at the Museum of Modern Art through Hemingway's suicide until it was eventually returned to Mary, who would subsequently lend it to the National Gallery of Art in Washington, where it found a permanent home.

That Miró painting was not the only piece of art that Hemingway possessed, just the one with the most intricate backstory. According to a piece for *DailyArt Magazine* by Zuzanna Stańska, Hemingway also owned several works by André Masson, including *The Throw of the Dice*, as well as Juan Gris's *The Guitar Player* and *The Bull Fighter*, which was also used as a frontispiece for *Death in the Afternoon*. René Villarreal also identifies *Monument in Arbert* by Paul Klee as being on display in the Finca Vigía (2009, 18). Another piece by Klee seems to have been in Hemingway's possession, too, as Hugh Eakin, in his essay on Hemingway and Miró's *The Farm*, writes of how "in 1936, Hemingway lent the Paul Klee he had bought with Pauline, *Monument under Construction*, to the museum's celebrated 'Fantastic Art, Dada, Surrealism' show" (2018).

Much of Hemingway's introduction to the art world came through his relationship with Gertrude Stein. Michael Reynolds recounts in his biography of Hemingway's time in Paris how "when Gertrude Stein said buy Masson, Hemingway bought Masson. When she said buy Miró, he purchased 'The Farm'" (*Paris Years*, 1999, 40). Hemingway also encountered art in its shifts and modernizations at Stein's salon where "between the tea and cakes, among the talk of who and where, [Hemingway] could see Picasso's blue period hung high on the wall, and his portrait of Gertrude with the face looking as much like Picasso as Gertrude. . . . [And] there were some fine Matisses left and plenty of Braque and Gris. And always Cézannes" (*Paris Years*, 1999, 40). In *A Moveable Feast*, Hemingway recounts how Stein "told us how to buy pictures[:] . . . buy your clothes for comfort and durability, and you will have the clothes and money to buy pictures" (2009, 25). In Stein's Parisian apartment, Hemingway remembers how "the pictures were wonderful and the talk was very good . . . about modern pictures and about painters" (2009, 26). The author's eye and interest in art seems to have been cultivated during those salons in Stein's Parisian apartment.

Colette Hemingway, an art historian with a PhD from Harvard University and the wife of Hemingway's grandson Seán, wrote a book on Hemingway as art collector, titled *in his time: Ernest Hemingway's Collection of Paintings and the Artists He Knew*. Colette Hemingway tracks the artworks Hemingway amassed over the course of his life and provides context into what drew Hemingway to these artists and the lives of the artists' themselves. That there is enough material to produce a work such as this speaks to the fact that it was no mere "myth" that Hemingway collected art.

Verdict: True.

Did Fidel Castro Use *For Whom the Bell Tolls* as a Guerrilla War Manual?

Thomas Bevilacqua

Hemingway's writing has had many afterlives. The author's literary works played different roles in shaping the world after he brought them into existence. How much of our concept of the 1920s comes from *The Sun Also Rises* (and, later, his memoir *A Moveable Feast*)? In the minds of many, Hemingway created a guide for the disaffected and disengaged who found the world around them lacking. Hemingway's "Big Two-Hearted River" was so associated with fishing that it was even republished in *Field and Stream* magazine. Hemingway's work provided these windows into certain times and worlds that would be essential to so many who hoped to explore them. One of the "guides" that Hemingway created, perhaps inadvertently, was in his novel of the Spanish Civil War, *For Whom the Bell Tolls*. The novel had an interesting afterlife as a guide for guerrilla warfare used in Cuba by Fidel Castro, which he acknowledged multiple times, even to Hemingway himself.

In *Hemingway's Havana: A Reflection of the Writer's Life in Cuba*, Robert Wheeler describes how "Castro would also credit Hemingway for teaching him the ways of guerrilla warfare through Hemingway's novel *For Whom the Bell Tolls*" (2018, 68). Valerie Hemingway, who was present at the one meeting between Hemingway and Castro, corroborates this. In her memoir, she recalls, "Ernest was pleased Fidel took that moment to let me know he was a reader and admirer of his work, especially *For Whom The Bell Tolls*. The strategy used by the guerrillas in the book had given him some ideas which he put to use when he was in the Sierra Maestra" (2005, 119). In an exchange between Castro and Kirby Jones (staff member on Robert F. Kennedy's 1968 campaign for the presidency) and Frank Mankiewicz (political adviser and press secretary for the same campaign), Castro again said "that Hemingway novel was one of the books that helped me plan the tactics with which to fight Batista's army," but the Cuban leader says that he "never told" Hemingway about this (quoted in Fuentes 1984, 174–75), contradicting what Valerie Hemingway and Wheeler have recorded.

In his autobiography, the Cuban ruler went into somewhat greater detail regarding what it was he learned from Hemingway's novel. Castro said that learning "the history of what happened at the rear during the Spanish Civil War was useful to us," specifically "knowing how the Republican guerrilla fighters behind the Franco forces managed to get their hands on the army's weapons" (2007, 209). Castro went on to stress the importance of how Hemingway "allowed" Castro "to actually *see* that experience" of guerrilla warfare, and he said they "always went back to it, consulted it, to find inspiration" (209). For someone who sought to go out into the world, to document what was happening in these places of great danger and conflict, it makes sense that Hemingway's work would in turn affect the strategy and decisions made by those leading a conflict. Though they were not friends, as so many would like them to be, Castro, like many of us, learned from Hemingway and his writing.

Castro's engagement with Hemingway's writing was not limited to reading *For Whom the Bell Tolls* and learning lessons about how to conduct a guerrilla insurgency. Castro also noted that he had "read some of his novels more than once," including *A Farewell to Arms* and *The Old Man and the Sea*, and said it was "the monologues, when his characters talk to himself" that the Cuban ruler "like[d] best" about Hemingway's writing (Castro 2007, 593).

Verdict: True.

Did an Infatuation Inspire Hemingway to Write *The Old Man and the Sea?*

Thomas Bevilacqua

Many factors led to Hemingway's composition of *The Old Man and the Sea*, the novella that would win the Pulitzer Prize and secure the Nobel Prize in Literature. Hemingway heard from Carlos Guitérrez, the original first mate on his boat *Pilar*, about an elderly fisherman who finally caught an enormous marlin over four days and nights only to see circling sharks eat the marlin's carcass before he could get it to shore. The way in which the literary public began to doubt Hemingway's ability after the failure of *Across the River and into the Trees* also was a motivating factor. "The American reviews bristled with such adjectives as disappointing, embarrassing, distressing, trivial, tawdry, garrulous, and tired . . . read[ing] like a parody of his former style," Carlos Baker recounts, as those reviews cast him, in Hemingway's terminology, as "a bum, hanging punch-drunk on the ropes" (1969, 486).

As that novel was what Jeffrey Meyers identifies as "the most personal and revealing of all Hemingway's novels" and as the author "never developed a detached, Olympian response to criticism [he] was deeply wounded by the negative reviews" (1985, 453). *The Old Man and the Sea* can also be understood as emerging from an affair of sorts with a much younger woman, one whom he fictionalized in the novel that led to the denigration of his literary reputation, *Across the River and into the Trees*. Hemingway's interactions and infatuation with Adriana Ivancich led him to write the work that would be the great capstone of his literary career.

Adriana came into Hemingway's world in 1948 when the author was in Italy, hunting at Baron Nanyuki Franchetti's lodge near Venice. It was a stop on Hemingway's first trip to Italy following the conclusion of World War II; "Fossalta was not far from Venice, and Ernest went to see the place where he had been wounded" (Dearborn 2017, 508). "With long, lovely black hair, green eyes, and a thin Roman nose," Michael Reynolds writes, "Adriana stepped into Hemingway's fantasy . . . certainly aware she had his full attention" (*Final Years*, 1999, 186). Hemingway's first journey to Italy since the end of the war, revisiting the place of a profoundly traumatic moment in his life as he approached his fiftieth birthday, perhaps primed him to be "smitten like a schoolboy" as he "fell in love with Adriana as soon as they met" (Meyers 1985, 452).

After their initial encounter, "Hemingway was finding it increasingly hard to resist her fresh, enticing beauty . . . overstep[ping] the boundary of propriety by inviting her for lunch the next day at the Gritti—just the two of them." The eighteen-year old, though "probably a little confused by Hemingway's attentions . . . was flattered enough to accept the invitation, against her mother's judgment," to this "milestone in their burgeoning relationship" (di Robilant 2018, 64–65).

Though questions about the nature of the relationship flew around, Adriana "was not attracted to [Hemingway] and could see, by reading [*Across the River and into the Trees*], that he had an unrealistic idea of the kind of woman she was" even as she "enjoyed Hemingway's generosity and love" (Meyers 1985, 447). They would correspond primarily through letters for "as with Agnes and with Hadley before their marriage," Meyers notes, "he spent very little time with her" (452). As this all transpired, Hemingway's wife Mary "thought he was a silly old man besotted with a teenager, and she . . . long waited for his infatuation to burn out" (Christian 2022, 226). Though what initially drew Ernest to Adriana was an intense romantic attraction to this gorgeous young Italian woman (and perhaps some reckoning with his own age), "the flirtation soon settled into a friendship" and "Ernest's growing affection extended to the Ivanciches as a family, especially when he met Gianfranco [Adrianna's brother], who had behaved so heroically in the war and suffered so profoundly" (Dearborn 2017, 511). Gianfranco also became someone with whom Hemingway would correspond through letters, even acknowledging the pain with which he struggled as he ended the suffering of one of his cats that had been hit by a car.

But beyond being an interesting and affecting moment in the author's biography, Adriana's presence and attention provided Hemingway with energy to write amid a time of great challenge. Adriana and her family's visit to Cuba and the Finca in late 1950 and early 1951 moved Hemingway as he "began writing what he thought to be the final section of the sea portion of the 'big book'— the story of an old Cuban fisherman's losing battle with a giant marlin" (*Final Years*, 1999, 237). Though that big book never came to pass for Hemingway, the kernel of what would eventually turn into *The Old Man and the Sea* began there and, to some degree, Adriana was the motivation and inspiration for writing. Brewster Chamberlin notes that Hemingway began writing *The Old Man and the Sea* in January 1951, with his first draft of the manuscript completed shortly after the Ivanciches left to return to Europe. Though "the one-sided passion of Ernest for Adriana was cooled by reality," Michael Reynolds recounts how "they would remain friends" and just as "her presence in his life had inspired *Across the River*," it also "set him free to write about an old fisherman's epic conflict" (*Final Years*, 1999, 238). "Ernest . . . still on a manic high, had been writing steadily since Adriana and her mother arrived," Mary Dearborn recalls. "[I]n fact, he later told Adriana that her presence made this stretch of work possible" (2017, 539), yet another example of how Hemingway "was neither the first nor the last of the romantics to elevate a pretty girl to the status of a muse while managing to remain in love with his wife" (Baker 1969, 488).

Adriana's imprint on *Old Man and the Sea* did not stop at its inspiration, as she also designed the cover art for the first edition of the book with the author "delight[ed]" that "Ivancich's dust jacket design . . . was accepted by Scribner's in lieu of the three covers he rejected" (Reynolds, *Final Years*, 1999, 250). Meyers contends that Hemingway "persuaded Scribner to accept Adriana's drawing and rigged the contest so that she would win" with Adriana's drawings described as being "so bad that we [at Scribner's] had to have them skillfully re-drawn [and] . . . what was on the jacket was not actually her original art, which was pretty abominable" (1985, 445). Ivancich was also responsible for the dust jacket for *Across the River and into the Trees*, the novel in part inspired by Hemingway's interactions with her.

This dynamic persisted until 1956, when Hemingway "received a letter from [Adriana]" that said she "had met a man who was keen to marry her" and "was also very jealous [and] forbade her to be in touch with Hemingway" (di Robilant 2018, 293). Explaining all this to Hemingway, Adriana wrote, "No tears, no words could make his mind change. I break now my promise to tell you . . . how very sad I am about this, how much I am attached to you and grateful for everything—that I will never never forget the wonderful days together and that I KNOW that you never meant or thought to do any harm to me" (quoted in di Robilant 2018, 294). While this relationship yielded multiple literary works, including one of the most important pieces of Hemingway's writing, "the personal . . . results were negative" as "it caused embarrassment to Dora [Adriana's mother] and Adriana, grief for Mary and frustration for Hemingway [who] behaved like a tame bear and looked like a fool" (Meyers 1985, 452).

Sadly, Adriana's connection to Hemingway affected the rest of her life. After Hemingway's death, she was plagued with difficulties that included multiple broken engagements and "an unhappy three-year marriage to an older Greek . . . who was intensely jealous and kept her locked up in the house" (Meyers 1985, 452). Her subsequent marriage to a German count "was also a disaster," as Adriana "became obsessed by Hemingway, fantasized about the past and was deeply disappointed by the failure of her book," which led to her being "hostile to her husband and alienated from her sons" (452). Mary Hemingway's memoir *How It Was* also cast Adriana as someone who "schemed to wreck the Hemingway marriage" (di Robilant 2018, 303). In addition to those issues, which would put an extreme strain on anyone's life, Adriana was also likely afflicted with a severe case of depression, and "her husband [who] seemed ill-equipped to deal with her mood swings and her withdrawals . . . became impatient [and] short-tempered" even as her "conditioned worsened," which included two attempts at suicide (303). Adriana, the woman who inspired *Across the River and into the Trees* and *The Old Man and the Sea*, took her own life on March 24, 1983.

Verdict: True.

Did Hemingway Attempt Suicide More Than Once?

Thomas Bevilacqua

Across the different milieus, the different arenas, the different spaces, one of Hemingway's central concerns in his writing is death. One need not look further than the short story "Indian Camp," the first story in the collection that announced Hemingway's presence on the modernist stage. This story features a Native American taking his own life due to his inability to tolerate the screams of his wife as she gives birth and closes with the young Nick Adams "sitting in the stern of the boat with his father rowing, [and] he felt quite sure that he would never die" (*Short Stories*, 2003, 95). Hemingway's work is full of destruction and death, quite often with intense examinations of how one faces the specter of death itself. Scott Donaldson observes how "it was not only the demands of craft that drove him to concentrate his gaze on death. . . . He had something to prove, and was for ever testing himself against danger. He climbed into the bullring during the amateurs, faced murderous animals in Africa, attended every war of his time. He put himself at risk, and he suffered the consequences" (1995, 288). As Hemingway physically and psychologically deteriorated, perhaps owing to the consequences of a life with such a focus, the push toward taking his own life as a way of ending his suffering appeared. We know how Hemingway's life eventually ended by his own hand, but leading up to that, there had been other attempts at suicide.

The impact of a life lived so dramatically and adventurously, coupled with a genetic predisposition to depression and mental illness left Hemingway in a diminished state by the time the 1960s began. In addition to doing things like "combing his hair forward to conceal his baldness" and having "nearly wept with frustration when he could not recall" certain facts (Baker 1969, 557), at this point Hemingway "wrote nothing," as he would "labor . . . all day, pausing only for lunch, covering scores of sheets, utterly unable to get it right" (559). His first wife, Hadley, noticed an "utter mirthlessness of his voice" (559) during a phone call as he worked to put together what eventually became the memoir *A Moveable Feast*. As his loved ones and doctors struggled to address his worsening condition, Hemingway was admitted into the Mayo Clinic in Minnesota, "where he was strapped down to receive numerous electroconvulsive shock treatments" that left him "shattered, unable to write." For though "the treatments alleviated his depression for a time," they also "wiped out the author's ability to create, stripping him of all purpose in the new year [of 1961]" (Feldman 2019, 342). This inability to write, which was rearing its head even before the electroshock treatments but that was really brought out through those treatments, hastened those feelings of uselessness and depression that resulted in attempts at suicide.

The first of these attempts occurred not long after the electroshock treatments that so damaged Hemingway's ability to write. Mary Dearborn recounts how she went downstairs "on April 18 [1961] . . . to find Ernest in a corner of the living room near the gun rack . . . holding a shotgun, and two shells lay on the nearest windowsill (2017, 624). Brewster Chamberlin records that on April 21, 1961, "EH attempts to shoot himself, but Mary talks to him for an hour until Dr. Saviers [George Saviers, Hemingway's doctor in Ketchum, Idaho] arrives [and] puts EH under heavy sedation"[21] (2015, 323). Mary "said that Ernest must not give up. He still had much do[,] . . . prais[ing] his courage[,] and [she] reminded him of his sons" (Baker 1969, 560), continuing to talk to him until Dr. Saviers arrived to defuse the situation. Andrea di Robilant even notes that "Mary found him in his red Venetian dressing gown" (2018,

300) as if to confirm the writer's assertion that "after their final fare-well[,] . . . both Hemingway and Adriana seemed unmoored without each other" (2018, 296).[22]

This suicide attempt was followed by another on April 23, and then on April 25, "at a repair shop in Rapid City, EH searches the hanger and automobiles for a gun and walks toward a taxiing airplane, whose pilot cuts the engines before EH can walk into the propeller" (Chamberlin 2015, 323). Those last two attempts occurred as Ernest and Mary and Dr. Saviers traveled to the Mayo Clinic in Minnesota for further electroshock treatment, as both Mary and Dr. Saviers realized that "Ernest would attempt suicide again if not readmitted to the Mayo Clinic" (Dearborn 2017, 624). Though they got him to the clinic for those additional electroshock treatments, the positive effects once again seemed to be only temporary and, at least in the eyes of Mary, were an example of Hemingway "put[ting] on an act of being in good mental health for the doctors" (624) so that he would be able to leave. Hemingway left the Mayo Clinic on June 26, but as Chamberlin notes, the author's "delusions return" on June 27 "and the trip [from the Mayo Clinic] becomes harrowing" (2015, 324). Things would get more harrowing upon Ernest and Mary's return to Ketchum, culminating with Ernest succeeding in taking his own life.[23]

While Hemingway's death, particularly the way in which it transpired, came as a shock to so many, knowledge of these attempts makes it seem not quite as shocking. Instead, the attempts reflect the constant pain Hemingway was living with during those years and his desire to end his life when it stopped being worth living. As Chamberlin records in the entry for the day when Hemingway took his own life, he was "dreading another day of antilife and the loss of everything that made him an individual human being with immense creative powers" (2015, 325). The conversations Hemingway had with friends during those later years also show that suicide might have been on his mind. One example comes from the recollection of Tillie Arnold, whom he had known from his life in Sun

Valley, Idaho. Tillie describes a time she "saw [Ernest] walking on the road" and "complaining about the incurable disease he had." Tillie "remembered a previous conversation in which Ernest had stated that suffering from an incurable disease would justify a person in taking their own life," and Hemingway confirmed that he was "referring to their earlier conversation" (Christian 2022, 286–87).

Verdict: True.

Did Hemingway Say, "There Is Nothing to Writing. All You Do Is Sit Down at a Typewriter and Bleed"?

Thomas Bevilacqua

Whenever one hears a quote that carries with it a certain aspect of pain and suffering, one often initially assumes it was said by Ernest Hemingway. This is the man who wrote, "But man is not made for defeat. . . . A man can be destroyed but not defeated" (Hemingway, *Old Man*, 2020, 66) and "If people bring so much courage to this world the world has to kill them to break them, so of course it kills them. The world breaks everyone and afterward many are strong at the broken places" (Hemingway, *Farewell*, 1995, 216). Hemingway was an author acutely attuned to the suffering and painful nature of life on this earth and what can come from it. As a writer, therefore, he could see applications of those aspects to his craft. That is certainly the case with the famous statement ascribed to Hemingway, "There is nothing to writing. All you do is sit down at a typewriter and bleed." Given the pain that comes along with suffering for the craft of writing, one can imagine Hemingway saying that.

The first attribution of this quote appeared, according to the work done by the website Quote Investigator, in William C. Knott's *The Craft of Fiction*, published in 1973. However, as Quote Investigator notes, "The earliest citations to the famous literary figures Thomas Wolfe and Ernest Hemingway occurred many years after their deaths. No supporting evidence was given, and the basic saying was already in circulation. Thus, there is no substantive evidence connecting the saying to Wolfe and Hemingway." So the quote frequently attributed to Hemingway does not appear to be something the writer ever said.

This quotation was also subject to an investigation on the Hemingway Society's blog by author Steve Paul. Paul consulted with Steven P. Gietschier, a professor at Lindenwood University in St. Charles, Missouri, and a scholar of both Hemingway and baseball. In that blog post by Paul, Gietschier notes:

The line about bleeding and writing is sometimes attributed to [Red] Smith although, like many quotations of this ilk, its origins are truly obscure. Walter Winchell, himself no mean journalist, wrote this in 1949: "Red Smith was asked if turning out a daily column wasn't quite a chore. 'Why, no,' dead-panned Smith. 'You simply sit down at the typewriter, open your veins, and bleed.'" Yet there is evidence that Paul Gallico, another sportswriter, used much the same language in 1946. (quoted in Paul 2016)

The Quote Investigator entry for this saying notes other places throughout the written record where elements of this phrase or its sentiment appear, but it states that all elements come together in the words of either Red Smith (via Walter Winchell) or Paul Gallico.

Much like the famous six-word short story, this construction and phrasing existed outside of Hemingway. But since it sounded like something that Hemingway might say (and attaching it to the legend of Hemingway would make it easier to use as a bit of branding), people decided that it must have been something he said.

Verdict: False.

Did Hemingway Suffer a Gunshot Wound While Fishing on the *Pilar*?

Thomas Bevilacqua

When one thinks of the injuries that could befall someone while out on a fishing expedition, one might think of some minor cuts and bruises or perhaps a nasty sunburn from being out in the sun all day. *The Old Man and the Sea* depicts all the different forms of physical suffering one can suffer while out at sea. As he struggles to catch the great marlin, Santiago reminds himself that he "know[s] how to suffer like a man" and "his hands were mushy" because of the struggle (Hemingway, *Old Man*, 2020, 59). But among all those different injuries one can easily suffer while fishing, gunshot wounds probably do not come to mind. Yet Ernest Hemingway found a way to get shot multiple times while out on his boat, *Pilar*.

James Mellow describes an incident that involved a machine gun. In 1935, while out with John Dos Passos and Michael Strater (a painter and friend of Hemingway's), "[t]he gun went off," Mellow writes, "and the bullet, ricocheting off the brass rail, struck Hemingway in the calves of both legs. They returned to Key West to get a doctor to dress the wounds," which "were not serious, having gone through the fleshy part of the legs" (1993, 465). In a piece for *Esquire* titled "On Being Shot Again: A Gulf Stream Letter," Hemingway went into extensive detail about this experience. In that piece, Hemingway recounts how he "end[ed] up shooting himself through both legs . . . while gaffing a shark" (Hemingway 1967, 199). While Hemingway held off a shark with his gaffing stick, he "shot [the] shark in the top of the head with the .22 caliber Colt automatic pistol shooting a greased, hollow-point, long rifle bullet[.] . . . [T]he gaff broke with a loud crack, the shaft striking [Hemingway] across the right hand, and, looking down[, Hemingway] saw that he was shot through the calf of the left leg" (Hemingway 1967, 201). Though the wound sent the crew on the *Pilar* back to Key West, "There was absolutely no pain at all" (202) that Hemingway could identify. Townsend Ludington's biography of John Dos Passos, one of the other guests on that fishing expedition, paints a slightly different picture. "Hemingway's wounds," Ludington writes, "began to give him pain and caused him to vomit into a bucket," and Hemingway "was humiliated by the accident," while Dos Passos's wife, Katy, "had no sympathy and was furious at [Hemingway] because of his carelessness and bravado" (1980, 348). Hemingway, ever conscious of the image of himself that he presented to the world, wanted to be sure he was seen as tough in the face of pain.

This would not be the only time Hemingway would incur a wound because of a firearm while out on the *Pilar*. Paul Hendrickson notes that Hemingway had "a tommy gun that he'd recently acquired from another Bimini fisherman" (2011, 226) on the *Pilar*. Katy Dos Passos provided a window into what it was like on the *Pilar* and what that gun was used for: "They come in like express trains and hit the fish like a planing mill. . . . Ernest shoots them with a machine gun. . . . It's terrific to see the bullets ripping into them—the sharks thrashing in blood and foam" (quoted in Hendrickson 2011, 228). Hemingway used the gun as a way of killing the sharks that would come after whatever fish he would catch while out fishing. But while the gun could be a useful tool for fishing in the Gulf Stream, it also resulted in another injury for Hemingway. This incident would also precipitate the end of Hemingway's friendship with Strater. Hendrickson noted that "Strater hooked a trophy black marlin" and "managed to get the fish close to the boat," but then Hemingway "started spraying the water" with that tommy gun he'd acquired, "bringing packs of sharks to *Pilar*'s stern," and by the time they were able to get the fish in, "most of its lower half [wasn't] there"

(2011, 226–27). However, the piece Hemingway would write for *Esquire* ("The President Vanquishes") on that fishing trip was missing "anything about [Hemingway] grabbing the tommy gun at the critical juncture to begin reddening the waters" as "it was jealous rage that made [Hemingway] do it, or so Strater would always believe. For the rest of his life, he'd nurse this grudge" (2011, 228).

Verdict: True.

Did Hemingway Write the Six-Word Short Story "For Sale: Baby Shoes, Never Worn"?

Thomas Bevilacqua

One of the best-known anecdotes is that of Hemingway being challenged to compose a story using as few words as possible. What Hemingway was alleged to come up with was "For Sale: Baby Shoes, Never Worn." It seems like a natural fit, the master of economic and direct prose creating a narrative that needed only six words to convey its emotion and power. The form itself, this very idea of creating a story in just six words, became a genre of its own and achieved a certain level of popularity. As David Fishelov notes, "It is evident that the mini-genre (or subgenre) of six-word stories has attracted, during the past decade, quite a few followers—both writers and readers. The magnitude and achievements of this new literary genre can be seen, for example, on the well-organized website http://www.sixwordsto-ries.net, which collects, selects, publishes, and categorizes hundreds of six-word stories" (2019, 31). One can look at the development of "flash fiction" from the six-word-story form as well as (for better or for worse) the emergence of Twitter and other microblogging platforms. While this has become an assumed portion of the Hemingway mythos, that the master of spartan prose was able to tell an entire story with emotional resonance using just six words, there's no evidence he wrote this story.

Quote Investigator investigated the question of this famous and extremely short story in 2013. The website identifies the origin of the quote and its association with Hemingway as coming from literary agent Peter Miller's 1991 book *Get Published! Get Produced!: A Literary Agent's Tips on How to Sell Your Writing*. As quoted in the Quote Investigator piece, Miller writes:

Apparently, Ernest Hemingway was lunching at Luchow's with a number of writers and claimed that he could write a short story that was only six words long. Of course, the other writers balked. Hemingway told each of them to put ten dollars in the middle of the table; if he was wrong, he said, he'd match it. If he was right, he would keep the entire pot. He quickly wrote six words down on a napkin and passed it around; Papa won the bet. The words were "FOR SALE, BABY SHOES, NEVER WORN." A beginning, a middle and an end!

While this anecdote is a perfect one to feature in a book by a literary agent about how to sell one's writing, and it fits perfectly with Hemingway's constrained style, there is little to no hard evidence that the story came from Hemingway himself. As Quote Investigator finds, one might find something like the story purported to be written by Hemingway in the classified sections of different newspapers. The Quote Investigator piece also notes the use of this construction, with either baby shoes or a baby carriage, that appeared in the classified section of newspapers dating back to 1910. Interestingly, Quote Investigator also tracks down a 1921 newspaper column by Roy K. Moulton, who, in discussing that construction, wonders, "Wouldn't that make a wonderful plot for the movies?"

Yet throughout this form's appearance in different mediums, there was a connection made with Hemingway, which seems to have come from John De Groot's 1989 one-man play, *Papa: A Play Based on the Legendary Lives of Ernest Hemingway*, that puts the six-word story in the mouth of Hemingway.

"'Bet you I can write a complete short story using only 6 words.

Any takers?

No?'

GRINS.

'Okay, then.

A short story in 6 words:

For sale.

Baby shoes.

Never worn.'

GRINS, PLEASED WITH HIMSELF."

This, per the work of Quote Investigator, is the earliest instance of the quote in print and attributed to Hemingway (though the Miller anecdote predates it, it was not put into print until afterward). Miller appeared to have taken the one-man play (and Hemingway's dialogue in it) as being from the figure himself and thus used the anecdote in his book.

Seemingly after this, the quote became associated with Hemingway, including in Miller's writing as well as in a piece written by the famed science fiction author Arthur C. Clarke that identified the phrase as coming from Hemingway's mind. All these things helped to calcify in the mind of readers that this story had been concocted by Hemingway.

Verdict: False.

Was Martha Gellhorn a Lesbian?

Thomas Bevilacqua

Martha Gellhorn, the third of Hemingway's wives, was something of an inspiration. She cannot be understood as anything less than a trailblazer for women, showing that they can put themselves into the same dangerous places as men and write about them just as effectively. Gellhorn's *New York Times* obituary articulates the impact she had, describing her "as one of the first female war correspondents [who] covered a dozen major conflicts in a writing career spanning more than six decades . . . a cocky, raspy-voiced maverick who saw herself as a champion of ordinary people trapped in conflicts created by the rich and powerful" (Lyman 1998).

The fact that she was such a "maverick," someone who did not fit into the idea of how a woman should act or what a woman should be interested in doing, allowed for questions or speculation about her sexuality and sexual orientation. While these questions that surround Gellhorn and certain aspects of her biography arouse interest or concern, ultimately the evidence we have seems to point toward Gellhorn not being what we would understand as a lesbian. One important thing to remember is that our present notions of sexual orientation are still new. Figures we now identify as "gay" might not have understood themselves as such. That said, there is evidence that Gellhorn's sexuality might now be understood as "queer" or not strictly adhering to the accepted norms of heterosexuality, which might have in turn fostered the belief that she was a lesbian. However, though there are questions, there's not enough in the way of true evidence to support the claim that Martha Gellhorn was in fact a lesbian.

Kenneth Lynn's Hemingway biography alludes to "some kind of incompatibility [that] may have marred Hemingway's sex life with Martha" (1995, 488), perhaps indicating that her sexual identity or orientation would not be understood as straight. "One of the great bonds in marriage—'with my body I thee worship'—was always lacking for Martha," Bernice Kert notes, which meant that "love-making could not provide the balm that softens so many marital quarrels," and that would have been particularly relevant given the "physical ardor" with which Hemingway pursued Gellhorn (1998, 382). Gloria Hemingway's memoir even alludes to "a basic sexual problem that explained a lot of their arguments" and that "could have been easily corrected by a visit to the doctor." But rather than do that, Ernest "tortured [Gellhorn] and when he had finally destroyed all her love for him and she had left him, he claimed she deserted him" (1976, 92). During their marriage, Gellhorn "found sexual relations less a matter of happiness" and more of "an awkward obligation" as "she had been astonished to discover . . . that making love was actually something women could enjoy" (Moorehead 2004, 198).

These issues of physical incompatibility might have shaped some of Hemingway's literary output. Lynn notes how *For Whom the Bell Tolls* depicts a "dream world" in which "erotic compatibility reigns" between Robert Jordan and Maria (Hemingway, *For Whom*, 1995, 488) while incompatibility dominated the relationship between Hemingway and Gellhorn at that same time.

These issues of sexual incompatibility might have been the result of other problems in the Hemingway-Gellhorn marriage, specifically Hemingway's feeling challenged by Gellhorn as a writer and war correspondent and the ways in which she challenged and existed outside more traditional gender roles. Early in their relationship, "Ernest tried to take charge of Martha" in such a way that "Martha wondered why she put up with such possessiveness," as "she was wary of any man who tried to take over," though "she never catered to him the way other women did" (Kert 1998, 297). While this dynamic functioned for a period, it was not one designed to last and seemed poised for a rather explosive dissolution. Mary Dearborn observes that their "marriage was effectively over when they traveled separately to Europe in May 1944" to cover World War II (2017, 444), noting that Hemingway "felt threatened by [Gellhorn's] refusal to stay home and take care of his needs[,] . . . object[ing] to her pursuing a career" (445). Initially, Hemingway seemed to accept Gellhorn's more pronounced role as "the writer in the family" but that was "doomed to fail, not because of her lack of talent but because of [Ernest's] compulsion to be Number One" (G. Hemingway 1976, 90–91). Though certainly not the only reason that the Gellhorn-Hemingway marriage did not last, Hemingway's frustration at how Gellhorn did not fulfill the more traditional and expected role of a woman in his mind seemed to have hastened the end.

One thinks of how Hemingway perceived the relationship between his mother and father and the role (at least in Hemingway's perception) his mother's emasculation of his father played in his deterioration and suicide. As Hemingway "identif[ied] with his father [and was] bitterly critical of his mother, the suicide set off a continuing search for a villain. Eventually he would cast Grace Hemingway in that role" (Kert 1998, 215). Hemingway possessed "the conviction that his mother had driven his father to suicide" (230), and that conviction seems based in the way his mother appeared to domineer his father, which seemed outside the standard masculine and feminine roles.

The nature of Hemingway's comments about Martha as he began his relationship with his eventual fourth wife, Mary, gives us a window into this thinking. He provided "shrill disparagements of Martha's coverage of the war [that] were ludicrous" (Kert 1998, 410). Perhaps it is telling that during this period in which his "deepest rage . . . was reserved for Martha," he could also be "heard . . . refer[ring] to Grace as 'that bitch' and speak[ing] of his father's cowardice" (Kert 1998, 409).

An incompatibility with Hemingway himself might have been based on any number of reasons and not indicative of Gellhorn being a lesbian, but in a time when things were not as closely understood as they are now, that incompatibility and any issues that arose might have been treated as signaling a lesbian identity. Amanda Vaill notes that Gellhorn "seemed uncomfortable in a maternal role," alluding to the "troubled" nature of her parenting of her adopted son, Alessandro (who was known as Sandy) (2015, 360). Biographer Caroline Moorehead recounts how "generally, [Gellhorn] found the boys [Sandy and his cousin] tedious and selfish and said that Sandy had the willpower of spaghetti" (2004, 341). There would be a period of estrangement between mother and son, as Sandy was "getting increasingly involved in the world of drugs . . . selling his few possessions and occasionally finding a few days' work as a waiter," and thus Martha's adopted son "became too ashamed and too afraid to make any further contact with Martha" (Moorehead 2004, 376). Perhaps owing to a more restrictive and stereotypical notion of gender roles and norms, Gellhorn's inability to fill the traditional roles assigned to heterosexual women might have led some to speculate and believe that she was a lesbian. Hemingway is alleged to have said that Gellhorn "write[s] so well and so poignantly" about children, yet she "don't give a goddamn about them" (quoted in Moorehead 2004, 198). However, Kert pushes back against this in *The Hemingway Women* when she describes how "the *Finca*" when Martha was there "came to seem like a paradise" for Hemingway's children, "with "the enchanting Martha, a new mother" (1998, 340). Moorehead notes how Gellhorn "had been genuinely fond of Hemingway's three sons and their bookish and competitive ways" (2004, 312). Observations such as these, coupled with the way in which Hemingway's son seemed noticeably sympathetic to her plight in his own memoir, seem to indicate that Gellhorn's lack of maternal instincts might not have been as pronounced as one might be led to believe. There was a period of estrangement between Martha and Sandy brought about by his involvement in the world of drugs that resulted in "Sandy [being] sent to prison, for drug possession and dealing" and then because "Martha did not approve of [Sandy's] marriage," and Martha viewed "her life with Sandy as a terrible chapter of failure" (Moorehead 2004, 376–77). However, though this period of estrangement was extreme, they would reconcile and "remained friends . . . for the rest of Martha's life," "they became close," and "the years of anger and resentment, if not redeemed, had at least been survived" (Moorehead 2004, 410). Martha's ability to forgive and allow for these resentments to subside, allowing for mother and son to remain close for the rest of the mother's life, speaks to a maternal instinct in Gellhorn that runs contrary to how some (including Hemingway) viewed her.

One can also look at the way in which Gellhorn thought and wrote about sexual activity and see how some might take that to be an indication of her sexual orientation. What appears in her more reflective work are views on sex that seem to be ambivalent and detached. Later in her life, Gellhorn wrote letters to her friend Betsy Drake about sex. She reflected upon how she "started living outside the sexual conventions long before anyone did such dangerous stuff" but that "to enjoy [sex] probably . . . seemed a defeat" for her and she "envied those who did [enjoy sex], realizing it made life so much easier" (quoted in Moorehead 2004, 408). Gellhorn recounts how "sex . . . seemed to be their [the male partner's] delight and all I got was a pleasure of being wanted, I suppose. . . . I daresay I was the worst bed partner in five continents" (quoted in Morehead 2004, 408). Gellhorn "had not enjoyed sex . . . until she was forty. . . . She had been to bed with men for many reasons . . . but not for desire" (409). These stumbling blocks, ones acknowledged by Gellhorn herself, toward physical intimacy with men could have been perceived, particularly by a world that did not understand the nuances of sexuality and gender, as being indicative of homosexuality. Terry Mort, in his book that tracks Hemingway's work as a correspondent, notes how "Martha makes it clear . . . that few, if any, of the many men in her life, before or after Hemingway, were able to arouse her physically" and that she "was a woman who maintained a certain emotional detachment in her personal life" (2016, 18–19). Sadly, one can imagine how this aspect of Gellhorn's personality, that "physical intimacy was not especially important to her" (Mort 2016, 19), could easily be reduced in more simplistic minds to being indicative of lesbianism. But the information we have at our disposal about Gellhorn and her life does not support the claim that the trailblazing writer was a lesbian.

Verdict: Improbable.

Did Hemingway Know a Prostitute Named Xenophobia?

Thomas Bevilacqua

El Floridita became well-known for introducing Hemingway to the daiquiri, which he became famous for loving. But also catching his eye and attention at El Floridita was the Cuban prostitute Xenophobia, who gained that moniker because she "had an aversion to foreigners" (Feldman 2011, 77). Paul Hendrickson describes how "[o] n Friday, May 5" Hemingway "collected a nineteen-year-old whore, whom he'd nicknamed Xenophobia" though "the trouble was she didn't like going to bed with her clients—so he liked to say" (2011, 325) as a way of allaying Mary's anger. But despite these assurances from Hemingway, when Mary returned to Cuba "the reunion . . . fouled when Mary discovered that, in her absence, Hemingway had had his teenage whore, Xenophobia, out to the house about three times" (Hendrickson 2011, 370).

In the volume of Hemingway's selected letters edited by Carlos Baker, Xenophobia appears twice, both in letters to Charles Scribner. In those letters, both written in 1950, Hemingway says, "We went into town and found Leopoldina and Xenaphobia [*sic*], after work done, and a couple or eight drinks and ran off the Killers which is quite a good motion picture until the very last," even saying, "I do not imagine this is the type of life which would have agreed with Henry James. . . . He wrote nice but he lived pretty dull I think" (*Selected Letters*, 2003, 703). In a subsequent letter, Hemingway describes how "Xenaphobia that kid I sent you the picture of has the old rale [syphilis] at 19 and has to be injected every afternoon at 1600. So it is sort of lonely about this joint. Naturally we will see that Xena is cured properly" (*Selected Letters*, 2003, 714).

Verdict: True.

Did Hemingway Manage a
Little League Baseball Team?

Thomas Bevilacqua

Among the many sports Hemingway loved was baseball. One thinks about how Hemingway uses the figure of Joe DiMaggio in *The Old Man and the Sea*. Santiago thinks to himself, "I must have confidence and I must be worthy of the great DiMaggio who does all things perfectly with the pain of the bone spur in his heel" (*Old Man*, 2020, 41). In the novel, DiMaggio functions as a figure of virtue and strength who guides Santiago during his struggle with the great marlin in a way that reflects an appreciation for that sport.

Robert Wheeler eloquently describes why Hemingway was so drawn to that sport in his book *Hemingway's Havana: A Reflection of the Writer's Life in Cuba*:

Baseball requires discipline and patience and to be in the right place at the right time in order to catch the ball; this is also true of fishing. One must keep one's poise in baseball and also on the sea, and one must be physically and mentally prepared for anything to come one's way. Hemingway knew that baseball and fishing demanded focus, and that both involved one's soul. This adds yet another dimension to Hemingway's novella and to his old man, Santiago. (2018, 24)

There is something about the game of baseball, how it is played, which drew Hemingway to it. Hemingway's interest in the game dates to his youth. Steve Paul recounts how Hemingway returned from Petosky, Michigan, to Oak Park, Illinois, "in time to revel in Happy Felsch's fourth-inning home run for the victorious Chicago White Sox in the first game of the World Series against the New York Giants" (Paul 2017, 8–9). Sharon Hamilton describes how, in 1921, "Hemingway was also living through circumstances painful to him as someone who had grown up as a fan of the Chicago White Sox" as "seven members of the White Sox were on trial in the nearby Cook County Criminal Court Building, accused of having colluded with gamblers to throw the 1919 World Series." Hemingway's time as a reporter for the *Kansas City Star* even allowed him to enter the world of Major League Baseball players; in 1918, he "caught the assignment to meet" with "two cars carrying the Chicago Cubs . . . to its spring training camp in Pasadena, California" including "Grover Cleveland Alexander, the pitching ace whom the Cubs had just purchased from the Philadelphia Phillies" (Paul 2017, 117–18).

Hemingway's love of baseball was not limited to that of the fan or to seeing it as another arena in which the ideas of courage and mastery he so highly valued could be put to the test. Hemingway also partook in managing a baseball team, specifically a Cuban Little League team, giving both his own children as well as Cuban children living in the area near the Finca Vigía experience playing the sport.

In an October 6, 2008, article for the *New York Times*, Joshua Robinson recounts how when Hemingway's two sons, Patrick and Gregory, were coming to Cuba in the summer of 1940, he was "not sure what to do with a 12- and an 8-year-old for that long, [so he] rounded up a dozen boys . . . to play baseball with them. . . . [J]ust inside the black and white gates of the farm, Hemingway set up an odd little ball field where he would pitch for both teams as they whiled away the hot afternoons." In that same article, Valerie Hemingway describes how "instead of shooing away [the young boys who would hang out near the Finca Vigía], Ernest found things for them to do . . . [and] when he knew Greg and Pat were coming, he started a baseball team" (Robinson 2008). This "baseball team for his sons and local boys that Hemingway organized in the 1940s" was known as "Gigi's All-Stars (or Gigi's Stars)," with Gigi being a nickname for Gregory, and might have been "the first young baseball team, baseball team with children, in the whole municipality" (Martens 2014, 30). During these games, Hemingway "used to pitch" and "bought each boy a uniform, a flannel uniform with stripes and a number in the back . . . [and] they were the first children to ever wear a baseball uniform in the whole municipality" (37).

Verdict: True.

Did Hemingway Leave a Penny in the Cement Next to the Swimming Pool at His Key West Home Because It "Took His Last Cent" to Build?

Thomas Bevilacqua

Take a trip to the Hemingway House and Museum in Key West, Florida, and you will see, at the home in which Hemingway wrote works such as "The Snows of Kilimanjaro" and "The Short Happy Life of Francis Macomber," a swimming pool shaded by numerous trees with many of Hemingway's beloved six-toed cats roaming nearby. The home, which was purchased by Hemingway and his second wife Pauline Pfeiffer in 1931, is a "Spanish colonial-style mansion . . . erected in 1851 by shipping tycoon Asa Tift . . . on a piece of property that included a large yard, a twenty-thousand-gallon cistern, and a carriage house that could be made into a secluded studio" (Hawkins 2012, 130–31). When the Hemingways purchased the home, it was in need of a great deal of renovation, but Pauline "was not constrained by finances, for Gus Pfeiffer [Pauline's uncle] had told Ernest and Pauline he would pay for it" (Dearborn 2017, 301). However, Hemingway's time living in Key West also saw the deterioration of his marriage to Pauline, as his romance with Martha Gellhorn, his eventual third wife, blossomed. To keep her husband happy, Pauline elected to have a swimming pool installed. That pool remains there to this day.

In the concrete near what was the first in-ground swimming pool built on Key West, you will find a single penny embedded in the cement. As the tour guides take groups through the grounds, you will hear them mention this curiosity before presenting a story of how Hemingway's then wife Pauline's construction efforts of this pool had taken his (metaphorical) last penny, which now in a more literal form forever stands in the concrete.

In a *New York Times* piece from February 2, 1964, titled "Hemingway House Becomes a Museum," we see the traditional story of the penny's origin reported: "On returning from a trip to Spain at that time, he remarked to the foreman on the job, 'I've spent my last cent on this pool.' Thereupon, he took a penny from his pocket and pressed it into the wet cement walk, where it still can be seen."

The Hemingway Home's website also provides some supposed insight into the penny's origins:

Ernest did complain mightily about the growing expenses of construction costs. Indeed, tourists who visit the property today are treated to humorous story [*sic*] of Hemingway, purportedly exasperated at the expense of the venture, flinging down a penny on the half-built flagstone pool patio and bellowing, "Pauline, you've spent all but my last penny, so you might as well have that!" Whether the story is apocryphal or not, there is a penny embedded in cement at the north end of the pool to memorialize Ernest's purported outburst. ("Our Gardens," 2021)

However, as the home's website notes with its careful use of the word "purportedly" and statement that the story might be apocryphal, the story may be more fantasy than reality. An *Atlas Obscura* article on the Hemingway Home and the pool notes the questionable sourcing of the penny story, and author Luke Spencer takes pains regarding the language used in the description:

Before the pool, the garden was home to Hemingway's own personal boxing ring, where he would train and spar with local boxers. Legend has it that whilst Hemingway was away working as a war correspondent during the Spanish Civil War, he fell in love with wife number three, fellow war journalist, Martha Gellhorn. Back in Key West, second wife Pauline Pfeiffer heard about the affair and replaced the author's beloved boxing ring with the pool out of spite.

The swimming pool was exorbitantly expensive for its time, costing over $20,000 in 1938. When Hemingway returned and found out about the costs, he supposedly flung the penny on the ground, saying "Pauline, you've spent all but my last penny, so you might as well have that!"

The cost of the pool, which was "two and a half times the purchase price of the house" (McIver 2002, 21), was certainly exorbitant, and according to Stuart McIver, Pfeiffer "retriev[ed] the penny . . . ha[ving] it preserved in cement and covered with glass, much to the delight many decades later of the sightseers Hemingway had hoped to keep at bay[,] . . . add[ing] a light touch to an absurd scene" (2002, 21). The irony, which McIver points out in his book, is that the money that went into the construction of the pool was not actually Hemingway's. Rather, it was Pfeiffer family money that paid for the pool, among other things. So it was not Hemingway's "pennies" that were going to fund its construction. Hemingway's exasperation and frustration at this enterprise were very real. Michael Reynolds notes that "on edge and ill-humored, Ernest found it difficult to be enthusiastic about the brick wall around their property or excavations for the newly begun swimming pool" (*1930s*, 1999, 282–83).

Carol Hemingway, who married Hemingway's son Patrick, recounts how "when Bernice Daniels bought the Whitehead Street house in 1961 [and] deciding to sell tickets and open it to the public

. . . she turned to Toby Bruce (and probably Betty), who were quick to make up stories that to their minds were colorful and corny, such as the fabrication about the 'last penny' spent on the swimming pool and the tasteless 'urinal' adapted for the cats drinking nearby" (2009, 39). Bruce, who had been friends with Hemingway for many years in Key West as well as his right-hand man/handyman, became a source for these anecdotes that would amuse visitors and imbue the home with a kind of charm. But while this narrative about the penny found in the poolside concrete is amusing and humorous, it does not seem to be true.

Verdict: False.

Did Hemingway Say, "The Typewriter Is My Therapist"?

Thomas Bevilacqua

Modern masculinity is wrapped up in an intense distrust for therapy and psychological introspection. One thinks of mob boss Tony Soprano sitting in Dr. Melfi's office bemoaning the loss of "the strong, silent type" best personified by Gary Cooper, who, incidentally, was a good friend of Hemingway's and starred in multiple film adaptations of his work. Though he predated *The Sopranos* by quite a few decades, Ernest Hemingway possessed a distrust of psychoanalysis and therapy that mirrored Tony's. As biographer Kenneth Lynn notes, the author was "adamantly opposed to seeking professional help in understanding" his psychological traumas (1995, 106). In a famous (or infamous) piece, Lillian Ross recounted how Hemingway hoped that sharing information regarding the struggles he endured while writing *The Sun Also Rises* would "encourage young writers so they won't have to go get advice from their psychoanalysts" and that he answered the question "What did [you] learn from psychoanalysts?" with "Very little" (2015, 59).

This is all intriguing to keep in mind as we engage with another entry in the "attributed to Ernest Hemingway" quote industry: "The typewriter is my therapist." One sees it pop up throughout Hemingway-centric discourse. For example, it appears in a 2013 *Atlantic* article on typewriters by James Joiner, who recalls that "Hemingway once told Ava Gardner that the only psychologist he would ever open up to was his typewriter." Irvin Yalom, a writer and psychiatrist, observed that "Hemingway . . . who always denigrated psychotherapy . . . acknowledged that his corona (i.e. his typewriter) was his psychiatrist" (2014, 248). Carl Eby references the quote at the beginning of his book, *Hemingway's Fetishism: Psychoanalysis and the Mirror of Manhood* (1998), while in a 2017 panel at the JFK Library, Andrew Farah (author of *Hemingway's Brain*) used the quote as well. We cannot say definitively that Hemingway uttered these words. But it's easy to imagine Hemingway making this statement based on a combination of the way in which the words ring true to Hemingway's own thinking (as opposed to "Write drunk, edit sober," which was addressed elsewhere in this book) and the way in which they have authoritatively appeared throughout the Hemingway discourse.

What perhaps distinguishes this quote from those other ones linked to Hemingway is the plausibility of the sentiment being expressed. Hemingway's views on psychotherapy, expressed throughout his life, reflect an extreme skepticism toward the practice. In addition, the importance the quote places on work (particularly the work of writing) seems to resonate with Hemingway's thinking. In those early years in Paris, when his life was "apparently hedonistic," he nonetheless was "follow[ing] a steady course of education and discipline, for he could not give himself up to pleasure if he had not completed his daily work. If he was not writing well or not writing at all, he became miserable and bad-tempered" (Meyers 1985, 67). The work of writing was vital to Hemingway, as it was instrumental to his ability to enjoy the other aspects of life. Hemingway's inability to write would be linked with his deterioration later in his life and might have prompted him to end that life. Though there is no definitive proof that this quote was indeed spoken by Hemingway, there is enough evidence to say that it was possibly uttered by him (while the other quotes documented in this book do not possess such a possibility).

Verdict: Possible.

Was Hemingway's Mother in Love with Another Woman?

Thomas Bevilacqua

Grace Hall Hemingway looms large in the narrative of the author's life. Even in this book, we have shown how her passion for music pushed Hemingway into playing the cello and noted Hemingway's belief that his mother's belittling of the man contributed to his father taking his own life. Grace is a major character in the Hemingway story. Some of the biographical and historical work on Grace has also alleged that Hemingway's mother might have been a lesbian. While there are certain aspects of Grace's history that lead to that speculation, evidence is circumstantial at best, and one cannot say with any degree of certainty that Hemingway's mother was, in fact, a lesbian and in love with another woman.

We see this notion in Kenneth Lynn's biography of the author, regarding a specific relationship Hemingway's mother had with another woman. Lynn describes "a quiet, attractive young woman in her early twenties named Ruth Arnold" who was "one of [Grace's] former pupils" that "moved into the Hemingways' Oak Park home as a part-time cook and mother's helper" (1995, 100). Lynn notes that "in the summer of 1919, Ruth accompanied Grace, Marceline, Ernest, and the younger children to Windemere," the Hemingway's cottage on Walloon Lake in Michigan, where Grace and Ruth "made rag rugs together and talked and sang" (100). Lynn writes of how "perhaps their relationship was sexually innocent; yet there is a 'malicious story' in certain quarters . . . that they were lovers" (100). Perhaps this "malicious story" is the reason why Ruth was given a rude welcome upon seeing Clarence Hemingway when she returned to Oak Park from Windemere. "Subsequent letters and replies" from Hemingway's father "make it clear that he banned Ruth Arnold from the Oak Park home" (Dearborn 2017, 82). James Mellow notes how some "have speculated that there may have been some taint of lesbianism in the relationship between Ruth Arnold and Grace Hemingway" (1993, 104), and that use of the word "speculated" seems key in assessing this.

Ruth's presence within the Hemingway household was not something that would have seemed strange. Mary Dearborn observes that "letters between Grace and Ruth during Grace's vacations away from the home indicate that Ruth played a part not unlike that of an au pair today, close to the children in age and often their friend as well as their caregiver" (2017, 81). This perception of Ruth's relationship also appears in the memoir written by Marcelline Hemingway Sanford, the author's sister, in which Ruth is described as Grace's "longtime friend" (Sanford 1999, 241) or as a kind of caretaker and helper around the home. Ruth Arnold remained a somewhat constant presence in Hemingway's mother's life up until its conclusion. Ruth was the one "who heard the shot" Hemingway's father took to end his own life "and told Grace when she returned to the house after an errand" before Hemingway's mother looked and confirmed what had transpired (Dearborn 2017, 267). Mary Dearborn notes that at some point after Ruth's husband, William Meehan, died in 1931, Ruth "went to live with Grace" (2017, 398) and would remain there until Grace's death in 1951.

In a letter Marcelline wrote to Ernest after the death of their mother, she recalls "how grand Ruth . . . was to Mother thru many many years" and that "Mother wanted to leave Ruth something equal to our shares in the will. She often talked of it" (Sanford 1999, 360–61), which reflects that the children understood the seriousness of the connection between their mother and this other woman.[24] Grace's children "often asked Grace to give their love to Ruth" (Dearborn 2017, 541) when they wrote letters to their mother as adults, evidence that Ruth was truly someone who was a part of the Hemingway family though not one accepted by Ed (Clarence) or later by Ernest, who never asked his mother to give Ruth his love at any point (Dearborn 2017, 541).

Lynn's biography of Hemingway highlights a potential connection in Hemingway's mind—possibly formed from Grace's relationship with Ruth Arnold—between Grace and Gertrude Stein. Beyond the fact that "in Oak Park 'Mrs. Stein' had been one of Hemingway's nicknames for his mother" and that "both liked to dominate conversations . . . in a contralto voice that commanded attention by its velvety loneliness as well as by its tone of assurance," Lynn highlights how "Gertrude's attachment to Alice Toklas" seemed to Ernest like "a bolder, Parisian version [of] his mother's relationship with Ruth Arnold" (1995, 168). Mary Dearborn, writing of Pauline's sister Jinny and her presence alongside Pauline and Ernest, describes how "Ernest just liked lesbians, perhaps remembering his mother's inclinations and her relationship with Ruth Arnold" before noting the different lesbians whom the author counted among his friends (2017, 250).

Because of the nature of their relationship, both in its intensity as well as in some of the reactions it elicited, questions still arise about Grace and Ruth Arnold's relationship. Though "we simply don't know whether Ernest (or his siblings) saw the relationship between the two women as a lesbian one" based on the correspondence it is clear that "Ed Hemingway clearly did" (Dearborn 2017, 85).

Verdict: Possible.

Did Hemingway Get in a Fight with Writer Wallace Stevens?

Thomas Bevilacqua

The lights in the fishing boats at anchor there,
As the night descended, tilting in the air,
Mastered the night and portioned out the sea,
Fixing emblazoned zones and fiery poles,
Arranging, deepening, enchanting night.

—Wallace Stevens, "The Idea of Order at Key West"

Hemingway was someone who could be goaded into a fight (see his first interaction with Orson Welles), and he could become particularly pugnacious when it came to contact with other literary figures. This was the case when, in late February 1936 (according to Brewster Chamberlin in *The Hemingway Log*), Hemingway found himself in the company of the poet Wallace Stevens. Stevens, who wrote a poem titled "The Idea of Order at Key West," found himself in that Florida city where he was able to "drink to excess, [which was] easy enough to do on the island that never recognized Prohibition" (Chamberlin 2015, 345). Paul Mariani describes how Stevens "had already been to the forty-year-old John Dos Passos's rented bungalow" and after the poet "stumbled over to another of Dos Passos's cocktail parties . . . joking and bantering with that dismissive edge of his . . . Hemingway's sister, Ursula . . . overheard Stevens insult her brother," as "he seemed suicidally itching for a fight" with the author (2016, 206).

After Ursula told Ernest what she had heard, Hemingway "confronted Stevens, a large man, a little drunk, a little belligerent, twenty years Hemingway's senior" (Reynolds, *1930s*, 1999, 221). The fight began with "Stevens swinging at the bespectacled Hemingway," but Hemingway was able to land two counterpunches (Mariani 2016, 207). After Hemingway was able to take off his glasses, Stevens did "[get] in a solid right to Ernest's jaw[25] before Hemingway put the poet down on the wet pavement, ending the fight" (Reynolds, *1930s*, 1999, 221). "Waldo Pierce saw [Stevens the] next day, wearing dark glasses to conceal the damage" (Baker 1969, 285) and eventually "a sober and chastened Stevens walked over to Hemingway's to apologize profusely . . . asking him to tell no one about the drunken brawl." Hemingway complied save for "crowing over the whole matter in a letter to Sara Murphy" (Mariani 2016, 208). Baker even refers to the fact that Hemingway "admired and respected Stevens as a poet" (1969, 285) as a way of explaining why the author did not broadcast the news of his brawl with Stevens.

The degree to which this story reads like something out of a Hemingway masculine fantasy gives one pause when it comes to accepting this as reality: the overserved poet besmirching Hemingway's good name and then punching Hemingway before he had a chance to take off his glasses, ending with Hemingway easily knocking out Stevens. Mary Dearborn notes how "only Ernest's version of what happened survives" (2017, 363), and Chamberlin reminds us that "no one is really sure what happened that night (or nights), and all the participants are dead, many having left no or some partial and distorted accounts of the fisticuffs" (2015, 345).

Hemingway's proclivity for fighting was certainly not a surprise. In addition to Stevens, Hemingway got into a fight with director Orson Welles (though the two would go on to become friends after the tussle), he hit Max Eastman in the face with a book according to a *New York Times* article titled "Hemingway Slaps Eastman in Face" from August 14, 1937, and he would frequently serve as James Joyce's protector when the Irish author's drunken provocations led to the threat of physical harm. In a 1954 article for *Time Magazine*, upon the success of *The Old Man and the Sea*, Hemingway was interviewed by Robert Manning, and he offered up the following anecdote: "We would go out and drink and Joyce would fall into a fight. He couldn't even see the man so he'd say: 'Deal with him, Hemingway! Deal with him'" (quoted in Ellman 1982, 695). Not only did Hemingway get into a fight with one of the great modernist writers, he also would get into fights on *behalf* of one of the great modernist writers.

Verdict: True.

Did Hemingway Commit Suicide by Putting a Shotgun to His Forehead?

Robert K. Elder

The method of Hemingway's death—whether he put a shotgun in his mouth or to his forehead—has been an unexpected source of disagreement among biographers. Why that detail matters is an important distinction of scholarship and how words and images resonate throughout culture. It also reveals how little we actually know about Hemingway's final moments.

Dr. Andrew Farah, the author of *Hemingway's Brain*, called the author's death "the most famous suicide in American history."

Actor Stacy Keach—who has portrayed Hemingway on stage and screen in addition to recording several audiobooks of the author's work—wrote that acting out the author's suicide in *Hemingway*, a 1988 TV miniseries, was unforgettable. "Without question, this death scene . . . was the most memorable for me, especially since I had spent months living inside the mind of the titanic personality and American icon," wrote Keach in a 2013 *New York Times* piece drawing on his biography *All in All: An Actor's Life on and off the Stage*:

✺

Ernest Hemingway's granddaughter Margaux came to the family home in Ketchum, Idaho, the day before we filmed this scene, but the set—which had letters bearing 1961 postmarks on his desk—felt so real, she could not bring herself to be there for the shoot. It was chilling for me as well, especially as I walked through his steps that day, laying down on his bed, walking into the kitchen to get keys, going out to the garage for the shotgun. Then I came back to the vestibule, closed the door and, finally, with my own nerves completely frayed by this experience, stuck the gun in my mouth.

This vulnerable, visceral image of Hemingway with a gun in his mouth has become iconic, much-referenced, and has inspired other works.[26] It also might be inaccurate.

But the story of *how* Hemingway killed himself at his home in Ketchum, Idaho, has been shrouded in privacy concerns and clouded by grief ever since the news broke on July 2, 1961. On that day, his fourth wife, Mary, initially issued a statement: "Mr. Hemingway accidentally killed himself while cleaning a gun this morning at 7:30 A.M. No time has been set for the funeral services, which will be private."

That story would quickly unravel, however, when the *New York Times* reported that the coroner said, "There had been no cleaning paraphernalia in evidence where he had been shot to death."

Mary would later recount that "the sounds of a couple of drawers banging shut awakened me and, dazed, I went downstairs, saw a crumpled heap of bathrobe and blood, the shotgun lying in the disintegrated flesh, in front of the vestibule of the sitting room."

At the behest of the family no inquest was held, and no autopsy was performed. Hemingway's death certificate, prepared by coroner Ray McGoldrick, would simply read: "Self inflicted gun shot wound in the head." In the section "Interval between onset and death," the entry reads, "Instant." The section for the coroner to fill in details about an "Accident, Homicide, Suicide" was left blank.

Other people who were present at Hemingway's death scene include coroner McGoldrick, Dr. Scott Earle and Chuck Atkinson, a local motel owner and friend of the Hemingways. Atkinson would take the suicide weapon, a 12-gauge shotgun, likely a W. & C. Scott Monte Carlo B, to destroy the gun before it became a prize for ghoulish trophy hunters.

It would take Mary another few years before she publicly admitted that her husband had committed suicide, and it would be decades before the full details of Hemingway's mental condition were widely known. Not only had Hemingway suffered multiple head traumas—including back-to-back plane crashes in 1954—but he had also been battling alcoholism, diabetes, and severe clinical depression that was being treated with electroconvulsive therapy at the Mayo Clinic. This was hidden from the public, as were his previous suicide attempts.

As for the exact method of his death, most scholars—including biographers Carlos Baker, Mary Dearborn, James R. Mellow, and Paul Hendrickson—have depicted Hemingway's suicide as a double-barrel shotgun blast to the *forehead*.

Jeffrey Meyers strayed from that story, however, in his 1985 book *Hemingway: A Biography*. He wrote that Hemingway "put the end of the barrel into his mouth, pulled the trigger and blew out his brains. . . . The carnage was much greater than [Mary Hemingway] suggests. Hemingway's chin, mouth and lower cheeks were left, but the upper half of his head was blown away. Blood, bones, teeth, hair and flesh were blasted around the ceiling, walls and floor of the room" (561).

The footnote for the entry, however, offers little illumination as to the source of his new forensic information, noting an interview with neighbor Tillie Arnold and strangely referencing "the photograph of a Spanish soldier with the top of his head blown off, which Hemingway reproduced in his article, 'Dying, Well or Badly,' . . . gives some sense of how he looked after the suicide" (620).

When I reached out to Meyers to ask for clarification and find out who his original source was, he declined to speak with me, citing other deadlines. When Meyers's source later revealed themself to me, they politely declined to talk. Moreover, they weren't an eyewitness, only a secondary source.

Yet biographer Michael Reynolds, who wrote a magisterial, five-volume biography of Hemingway, concurred with Meyers's version of events.

In 1999's *Hemingway: The Final Years*, Reynolds wrote that Hemingway picked up his favorite shotgun, "slipped in two shells and snapped the breech shut. The taste of gun oil and powder solvent filled his mouth as cold steel made contact against his hard palate. The clock on Mary's bedside table clicked as the minute hand moved to 7:30. Then two, almost simultaneous explosions woke her to her widowhood, her world changed, utterly changed" (359).

While Reynolds's prose is elegant, it still falls under the category of dramatization. But Meyers's and Reynolds's conclusions are bolstered by two accounts of Hemingway entertaining guests with an elaborate scenario of suicide with a gun in his mouth.

"Look, this is how I'm going to do it," Hemingway told his dinner guests in Cuba, as recorded in Kenneth Lynn's controversial biography *Hemingway*, originally published in 1987 (582).

Hemingway would "sit in his chair, barefoot, and place the butt of his Mannlicher .256 on the fiber rug of the living room between his legs . . .[and,] leaning forward, he would rest the mouth of the gun barrel against the roof of his mouth," friend Dr. Jose Herrera told Lynn. "He would press the trigger with his big toe and we would hear the click of the gun" (583).

"This is the technique of harakiri with a gun. . . . The palate is the softest part of the head" (583), Hemingway told Herrera and gathered friends.

Rene Villarreal, the head of Hemingway's household staff, told a similar story in his 2009 memoir, *Hemingway's Cuban Son*. Hemingway used to tell friends at his home in Cuba "how he would blow off his head with a shotgun by placing it in his mouth and tripping the trigger with his big toe," Villarreal wrote (135).

Even with these sources, Lynn acknowledged the uncertainty surrounding the details of Hemingway's death. "The explosion blew away his entire cranial vault," Lynn wrote (1995, 592). "Whether he had placed the gun barrels in his mouth or pressed them to his forehead is impossible to say."

But there's more to explore here. As for the forensics of the suicide, only a few biographies make reference to teeth being among the viscera left in the foyer, which might give credence to the story of a shotgun blast to the mouth. But that detail seems to have been added by biographers from previous accounts and not attributed to known firsthand accounts.

In his 2016 biography *Ernest Hemingway (A New Life)*, James M. Hutchisson wrote that "bone, teeth, hair, and flesh were scattered around the floor and stuck to the ceiling" (2016, 248).

In *Hemingway's Boat*, biographer Paul Hendrickson described what Dr. Earle—the second person on the scene—experienced as he saw "fragments of strewn bone, teeth, hair, flesh. . . . The walls and the ceiling and floor of the boxlike space were 'speckled,' the doctor said, with a yellowish red. Hemingway's legs were 'flexed,' and between them, resting against his chest, was the double-barreled 12-gauge" (2011, 456).

But in tracking down Hendrickson's original source—two handwritten and two typed pages of Baker's interview notes with Dr. Earle, now in the Special Collections Department at Princeton University—there is no mention of teeth.

"The entire cranial vault had been blown off by a double blast from the shotgun," Baker wrote. "The face below it was a bloodless caricature. The disc-shaped and empty skull was visible from the living-room."

These grisly details, taken from Dr. Earle by Baker, suggest that Hemingway didn't stick the shotgun in his mouth—simply from the observation that the body had a face that wasn't destroyed in the blast and there were no teeth at the scene.

Baker's notes are precise and even include the dimensions of the hallway (7½ feet x 5½ feet). Using Earle as the primary source, Baker wrote that Hemingway pressed the muzzle of the gun "against his forehead just above the eyebrows."

I shared my findings with Dr. Ryan D. McCormick, the associate medical examiner at the Hillsborough County Medical Examiner

Department in Tampa, Florida. Dr. McCormick—who is board certified in forensic pathology, anatomic pathology, and clinical pathology—provided a thoughtful and detailed response. A brief warning here to those who are sensitive to crime scene descriptions and suicide.

On the Lack of Teeth at the Scene

"Soot within the mouth, a defect to the palate, a laceration of the tongue, and small lacerations of the skin circumscribing or at the corners of the mouth are all signs that would suggest an intraoral entrance wound. Teeth being present at the scene would also be something that would lead me to consider an intraoral wound," he wrote.

But since there is no reliable firsthand report of scattered teeth at the death scene, it casts doubt on Hemingway committing suicide via a gun in his mouth.

Was the Entry Wound on the Forehead?

It's complicated, Dr. McCormick wrote.

"In a contact wound of the forehead, one would expect to see a muzzle stamp. The muzzle stamp is an imprint of the muzzle where it was in contact with the skin at the time the weapon was discharged. The muzzle stamp may not be obvious and sometimes requires a close examination of the entrance wound to find," he wrote. "There is no information to suggest any of these findings in Dr. Earle's interview."

Condition of the Head

One detail that did catch Dr. McCormick's attention was Dr. Earle's description of the "disc-shaped and empty skull."

"In my opinion, this is specifically referring to the base of the skull, where the brain sits in the cranial cavity. It has a round-to-oval shape. In intraoral shotgun wounds, the projectiles and gas enter through the base of the skull fracturing these bones into small pieces," wrote Dr. McCormick. "In my experience, when looking into the skull the 'disc' shape tends to not be maintained. A contact wound of the forehead may cause some fracture of the base of the skull, but the shape does tend to be retained."

While this appears to lend more credence to the forehead hypothesis, Dr. McCormick cautioned, "Without more details, I am uncertain the location will ever truly be known."

But there is always more research to be done and more sources that have yet to be discovered. Dr. McCormick suggested that "exhumation could potentially answer the question depending on the condition of his remains. It would at least give a forensic pathologist the chance to examine his injuries and answer the question."

But that is likely out of the question.

"It was a closed-casket ceremony, which made up for the fact that no morticians could have dealt with the challenge of an open-casket funeral," Hemingway's son, Patrick, wrote in *Dear Papa: The Letters of Patrick and Ernest Hemingway* (2022). "What lay in the coffin could hardly be called the grace of a happy death" (P. Hemingway 2022, 306).

Verdict: Probable. Baker's original report, bolstered by his interview with Dr. Earle, is the most correct. Hemingway most likely did place the shotgun that killed him to his forehead.

Did Hemingway Have Clinical Depression and Suicidal Tendencies on Both Sides of His Family?

Robert K. Elder

Until recently, that was uncertain.

But a letter found in River Forest, Illinois, from Hemingway's maternal uncle, Leicester C. Hall, sheds new light on the family's history with depression.

The darkest, most haunting part of the letter comes in the middle.

"I had several seconds of complete blackness a few weeks ago," wrote Hall, describing a moment of catatonic paralysis. "I made several attempts to open my eyes. They seemed to be sealed. Finally I seemed to make a final despairing effort . . . and I came back. No pain, no joy, no grief, mental or physical, during the struggle. I don't know whether it was a foretaste of death or only a dream."

This newly discovered letter sheds light on the Hemingway family's generational battle against clinical depression.

Dr. Andrew Farah, author of *Hemingway's Brain*, called Hall's letter "fascinating."

"When we see depression with catatonia, we often are dealing with a bipolar illness," says Farah, who serves as the chief of psychiatry in the High Point Division of the University of North Carolina Healthcare System.

"It certainly confirms and solidifies that understanding that there was a genetic basis for the depression," Farah says.

This letter, along with a small trove of Hemingway family documents, was brought to my attention by James R. Hopkinson, a Chicago attorney, who bought Hemingway's mother's house in River Forest.

Hall likely sent the letter in 1943 or 1944 to his sister Grace Hall Hemingway, the mother of Ernest. Hall identifies himself as seventy years old at the time.

He seemed to have some difficulty composing the letter, which is typed on one and a half pages of his letterhead.

"My mind, (what is left of it), goes blank when I try to write a personal letter," Hall wrote his sister. "For several months I have been carrying around with me in a brief case your last three letters ... hoping against hope that I might have some inspiration or mental uplift from the sordidness of existence that I might write something encouraging to you. No luck."

In Hemingway family lore, Leicester Hall was a figure of adventure, entrepreneurship, and tragedy. Hall was also the namesake of Hemingway's only brother, Leicester. Relatively little has been written about him in Hemingway biographies, but a few details have surfaced:

Hall was the beloved only brother of Grace Hemingway, and she wrote at least one piece of music in his honor, "The Leicester Waltz." Hall was a graduate of Amherst College, a Greek scholar, an amateur musician, and a thrill seeker who braved the winters of Alaska to search for gold in the Yukon.

He was a supply officer in an aero squadron during World War I, but he went missing in action in 1918, possibly taken by the Germans as a prisoner of war. By December of that year, however, Hall had been accounted for and was sent back to Allied soil.

When he returned to the United States, however, Hall found that his wife, Nevada Butler Hall, had died of influenza. After the war, Hall settled in Bakersfield, California, where he practiced law. By 1949, after this letter was written, Hall started to suffer from chronic insomnia.

This letter is also notable because it serves as evidence of clinical depression on both sides of Hemingway's family. The only previous link had been a family story told by Marcelline Hemingway Sanford in her family history *At the Hemingways* (originally published 1962), about a suicide attempt made by her grandfather, Leicester Hall's father.

"Clearly, if one parent or one grandparent has depression or bipolar disorder, it certainly increases the risk to descendants. But if you get it from both sides, it is a magnified risk," Farah says.

The legacy of suicide seemed to permeate Hemingway's world. The author's father, Clarence Edmonds, killed himself in 1928 with a pistol. Hemingway's maternal grandfather attempted to kill himself, and the author's sister Ursula and brother Leicester both ended their lives in 1966 and 1982, respectively. Moreover, the number of suicides in his social circle and bloodline are striking—his third wife, Martha Gellhorn, his granddaughter Margaux, his first wife's father, and many more. Themes of death and self-destruction permeate his fiction, journalism, and correspondence.

After his father killed himself, Hemingway wrote to his mother-in-law, Mary Pfeiffer, saying, "I'll probably go the same way." But Hemingway's suicidal ideation predated his father's death in 1928.

In a notebook dated March 6, 1926, Hemingway wrote a three-page meditation on death—including thoughts of suicide. At the time, the budding author was just twenty-six, and seven months away from publishing *The Sun Also Rises*, his first major novel.

"When I feel low I like to think about death and the various ways of dying and I think probably the best way, unless you could arrange to die some way while asleep, would be to go off a liner at night," he wrote in the book, which is now part of the Toby and Betty Bruce collection of Ernest Hemingway in the Penn State Special Collections Library.

He continued: "For so many years I was afraid of death and it is very comfortable to be without that fear. Of course it may return again at any time."

Hemingway appeared to have second thoughts, however, and later added a handwritten coda in pencil. "This is horse shit," he declared.

In 2017, Dr. Farah wrote that Hemingway had been misdiagnosed as bipolar, when he actually suffered from chronic traumatic encephalopathy (CTE), a brain disorder most associated now with professional football players. This misdiagnosis, Farah contends, only accelerated Hemingway's self-destruction.

The fact that this letter identifies clinical depression on Hemingway's mother's branch of the family is both illuminating and disturbing.

"Reading it again, it was just so sad. At first, I had no idea who Leicester was," says Hopkinson, who moved into Mrs. Hemingway's former River Forest home. The letter, and a few other family artifacts, came with the house.

Grace moved into the house at 551 Keystone Avenue in 1936 and lived there until her death in 1951. She used the property's large garage studio to pursue her hobby of painting landscape canvases, a few of which were left behind after the sale by the Hemingway family, along with some furnishings and the letter from Leicester.

Hopkinson and his family have since moved out of the River Forest home, but he hopes that the material adds something to Hemingway scholarship and helps people understand the family's struggle against clinical depression.

"I thought it had passed from father to son, but clearly his uncle is suffering from the same despair," says Hopkinson.

And yet, Hall showed bravery in facing his own mortality.

In a sentiment he attributes to the historian Lewis Mumford, Hall writes that "the greatest glory and triumph a man can have is to face inevitable disaster without flinching."

Verdict: True.

Did Hemingway Say That His Hometown of Oak Park, Illinois, Was a Place of "Wide Lawns and Narrow Minds"?

Robert K. Elder

It's a very compact, Hemingwayesque line, repeated often in Oak Park. But there's no record that Ernest Hemingway ever said—or wrote—that his hometown was a place of "wide lawns and narrow minds." Not in books, interviews, short stories, diaries, articles, or letters.

But the line was so memorable that Hemingway's first biographer, Carlos Baker, referenced it in his *Ernest Hemingway: A Life Story* (1969). But even Baker couldn't verify the quote.

"We've never found it," says Rose Marie Burwell, scholar and author of *Hemingway: The Postwar Years and the Posthumous Novels*.

However, Burwell thinks the line expresses what Hemingway saw as "the narrowness of the social and religious teachings that were so dense in his home."

Often, his frustration seemed to be with his family, rather than Oak Park itself.

In his early letters, Hemingway expressed a fondness for friends and family in Oak Park. In fact, he participated in school plays and varsity football and was declared "class prophet" in his high school yearbook. As an ambulance driver in World War I, he told a friend that he was from Oak Park, near Chicago: "Way out where the West begins." When he was wounded in 1918, he sent letters home asking for copies of his high school newspaper *The Trapeze*, and the *Oak Leaves*.

He even came back to Oak Park to speak about his war experiences and was treated as a hero. The March 22, 1919, edition of the *Oak Leaves* recounted a nervous Hemingway's address to his high school.

"Anybody who says he wasn't scared in this war was either a liar or else wasn't in it," he said. "One way a soldier has of telling he is scared is that he can't spit. I couldn't spit right now to save myself."

Then, of course, the twenty-year-old Hemingway regaled the crowd with tales of his own heroism and the horrors of trench warfare.

But his relationship with his parents became tense after he started publishing fiction.

His father, Dr. Clarence Hemingway, sent back all six copies of the 1924 Paris edition of his son's autobiographically inspired short story collection *in our time*. His parents were particularly horrified by their son's matter-of-fact prose about a war veteran catching gonor-rhea from a salesgirl in the back of a Lincoln Park taxi. Dr. Heming-way said he would not tolerate "such filth" in his house.

"Trust you will see and describe more of humanity of a different character in future," the doctor wrote to his son. "Remember God holds us each responsible to do our best."

Later, Hemingway jokingly wondered if the US edition of his book would be "burned on the steps of the O.P. Library," in a 1925 missive reprinted in *The Letters of Ernest Hemingway: Volume 2, 1923–1925*.

Tensions with his family boiled over when Hemingway's first novel, *The Sun Also Rises*, made him a literary star in 1926. His mother, Grace Hall Hemingway, called it "one of the filthiest books of the year" and objected to his use of foul language.

"What is the matter? Have you ceased to be interested in loyalty, nobility, honor and fineness in life?" she wrote him. "Every page fills me with a sick loathing—if I should pick up a book by any other writer with such words in it, I should read no more—but pitch it in the fire."

In reply, Hemingway defended himself in a letter to both parents: "I am in no way ashamed of the book, except in as I may have failed in accurately portraying the people I wrote of, or in making them really come alive to the reader. I am sure the book is unpleasant. But it is not all unpleasant and I am sure is no more unpleasant than the real inner lives of some of our best Oak Park families."

Nancy Sindelar, author of *Influencing Hemingway*, said Hemingway's relationship with Oak Park and his parents was complicated.

"He had a work ethic all his life because of his parents. He got a fabulous education in the Oak Park schools, and his parents were very loving, but very strict," said Sindelar (Elder 2014).

Hemingway was hurt by his family's reaction and lack of acceptance of his early work, Sindelar said, "But later on they did accept it."

In 1929, Hemingway's mother applauded his book *A Farewell to Arms* and included positive press reviews in a letter. She wrote to her son: "It is the best you have done yet and deserves the high praise it is receiving."

Verdict: False.

Did Hemingway Kill 122 Nazis during World War II?

Robert K. Elder and Mark Cirino

Chris Kyle, the soldier of *American Sniper* fame, was credited with 160 kills, a record that made him the deadliest military sniper in American history, surpassing the previous record of 109 confirmed kills.

But Ernest Hemingway might have challenged those records, according to his own accounts. Hemingway repeatedly told friends that he killed 122 enemy soldiers during World War II. If the author's claims are to be believed, then the original American sniper might have been Hemingway, a *Collier's* magazine correspondent who, according to the Geneva Conventions, was not even permitted to hold a weapon.

Yet Hemingway regularly boasted to people such as Marlene Dietrich and Pablo Picasso that he had been wounded sixteen times and had killed 122 men.

In October 1950, in a letter to author Evelyn Waugh (*Brideshead Revisited*), he wrote that the figure wasn't such an impressive total, "especially for anyone who had ever have [*sic*] to teach sniping."

Although Hemingway was an excellent and devoted hunter, there is no evidence that he ever instructed soldiers in the art of sniping.

Hemingway's self-perpetuated image was often at odds with the historical record, not to mention common sense. Hemingway saw three wars—first, as an American Red Cross volunteer in World War I and then as a journalist during the Spanish Civil War and World War II.

Hemingway viewed D-Day operations on June 5–6, 1944, and transferred to the Fourth Infantry by the end of July. He traveled back and forth from the front until leaving for Cuba in March 1945. Hemingway's greatest exposure to combat would have been Rambouillet in August, Belgium in September, and the Battle of Hurtgen Forest in November.

As Hemingway grew comfortable with military leaders, particularly the Twenty-Second Infantry Regiment commander Buck Lanham, his nonjournalistic activities during the war started to draw scrutiny.

On October 6, 1944, Hemingway was called before the army inspector general following his actions in Rambouillet in late August, when Hemingway "liberated" the Ritz Hotel with partisans. This interrogation led to the memorable exchange:

Inspector General: Were there mines in your room?

Hemingway: There were no mines in my room. I would greatly prefer not to have mines in my room.

In front of the inspector general, Hemingway denied behaving as anything other than a journalist, which he later regretted. Even after this inquiry, Hemingway privately portrayed himself as an active participant in hunting "Krauts" in September 1944, during the Hurtgen Forest campaign.

In his private journal, Hemingway wrote that he had to shoot a German soldier "three times before he stopped."

"I was in back of the pill box and I ~~killed the one~~ shot the one in back of us across the road in the woods about 15 yards," Hemingway wrote.

It's notable that he changed "killed" to "shot" in this passage, either opting for precision in description or choosing a more conservative means of recording the experience.

When comparing "kills," context is important. American sniper Kyle, whose own credibility has been called into question, nevertheless had 160 kills confirmed by the navy in his ten-year career. By contrast, Hemingway claimed to have killed 122 enemy troops in three months of intermittent engagement with the enemy.

After World War II, Hemingway began to include the number 122 in his work.

In *Across the River and into the Trees*, Hemingway's first novel after the war, his dying protagonist Colonel Richard Cantwell tells his young Italian girlfriend that he has, indeed, killed armed men: "One hundred and twenty-two sures. Not counting possibles."

In his posthumous novel, *Islands in the Stream*, painter-turned-solider Thomas Hudson recollects the story of Colonel Crittenden and the 1851 expedition to Cuba, which resulted in a mass execution by the Spanish army. Hudson remembers, "They had shot one hundred and twenty-two American volunteers" against the hill of Atares in Bahía Honda. The number Hemingway chooses is striking, particularly when considering that the actual historical number of executed was fifty.

But the first casualty of war is the truth, as Hiram Johnson pointed out. For Hemingway, the line between fact and fiction is a point of tension, both in his work and in his life.

Hemingway biographer Michael S. Reynolds wrote that the number of Hemingway's wartime victims "increased in direct ratio to his drinking" (*Final Years*, 1999, 154).

Leicester Hemingway, Ernest's younger brother, thought that "any number in excess of a hundred is really putting a gloss on it," nevertheless allowing credence to his brother's claim.

Hemingway's son John was more noncommittal: "I suppose he killed some," he said.

Charles Whiting—whose *Hemingway Goes to War* chronicles Hemingway's World War II activities—was more critical. He derided Hemingway as "simply a tourist in a helmet."

When we asked author Tim O'Brien, a Vietnam veteran and author of *The Things They Carried*, about the story, he offered this reaction: "122? That's a preposterous number. How do you *confirm* even a single kill? War is chaos."

"I'm not sure if he killed anyone," said O'Brien.

But it was perhaps Pablo Picasso who had the most insight.

When Hemingway and Picasso dined together after World War II, Hemingway presented Picasso with materials he had purportedly taken from a Nazi he had killed.

"He came to see me after the Liberation and he gave me a piece of an SS uniform with SS embroidered on it, and he told me that he had killed the man himself," Picasso recounted. "It was a lie. Maybe he had killed plenty of wild animals, but he never killed a man. If he had killed one, he wouldn't have needed to pass around souvenirs."

Verdict: False.

Is It True That Hemingway Didn't Date and Wasn't Interested in Girls in High School?

Robert K. Elder

This story about Hemingway is a longstanding misconception, mostly because it comes from his own high school classmates.

"He preferred to go hunting and fishing. If any classmate can say he ever saw Ernie take a girl to a dance or a school party . . . I don't know who that person was," wrote classmate Susan Lowrey Kesler in the booklet *Ernest Hemingway as Recalled by His High School Contemporaries.*

Even his school friend Lewis Clarahan said that Hemingway "did not care to date and seemed to avoid girls."

But through some research and original reporting, I found this distinctly not to be the case. In fact, Hemingway was interested in and pursued at least three high school girls—he even wrote a poem to one of them saying: "I'd gladly walk thru Hell with you / Or give my life."

Here, we explore each of Hemingway's high school love interests and how they impacted his life and work.

Annette DeVoe

"Your Matchless grace/your sensuous loveliness and your beauty strikes me dumb," wrote a teenage Ernest Hemingway.

While working on the book *Hidden Hemingway: Inside the Ernest Hemingway Archives of Oak Park,*" I found this poetry fragment among some of Hemingway's high school assignments in a vault at the Oak Park Public Library. Initially, it seemed like a draft of a poetry assignment, but an enlarged image revealed two other details. First was the line "Oh god I love you" and second was a name: "Annette."

None of the biographies mentions Annette, and Hemingway names her only a handful of times in his early letters—sometimes in clandestine terms.

In an undated note to an unnamed friend, the young Hemingway wrote, "Tonight maybe, any time we can get together. How about it? The river is good and high now. When shall we pull off our trip with A.D.V. and C.M."

A.D.V. was Annette DeVoe, a junior who worked with Hemingway on his senior yearbook, the *Tabula*, according to *The Letters of Ernest Hemingway: Volume 1, 1907–1922*. She would have been a junior when Hemingway was a senior at Oak Park and River Forest High School. A staff photo for the *Tabula* shows her cherub-faced and smiling. She's not standing next to Ernest but to Marcelline Hemingway, his sister.

On January 8, 1918, Hemingway wrote Marcelline from Kansas City, where he was working as a cub reporter after graduating high school. On *Kansas City Star* stationery, he asks for gossip from a recent party: "Who was there (and) what did they do and did they ask for me and what did they say and have you seen Annette?"

Buried in a footnote in Hemingway's correspondence, Marcelline compliments her brother on "picking winners," in a reference to Annette and their classmate Frances Coates.

Annette appears only a few more times in his correspondence. Whatever their relationship was—or if he ever sent her the poem— it's clear that Annette was a romantic touchstone for him, a standard by which other women were compared.

Another line from his poem reads: "I'd gladly walk thru Hell with you / Or give my life."

For anyone who ever fell in love in their teens, no matter the century, it's easy to empathize. To the inexperienced heart, love can be an elemental force, like gravity. You can float or get crushed under its weight.

The following year, other forces pulled at Hemingway. While serving as a volunteer ambulance driver in World War I for the American Red Cross, Hemingway was wounded during a mortar attack on the Italian front. While recovering, the nineteen-year-old Hemingway fell in love with his nurse, Agnes von Kurowsky.

On November 11, 1918, he wrote Marcelline that "A. DeV. and all other(s) can take a back seat" to von Kurowsky.

In the same letter, he wrote, "I don't wear my heart on my sleeve anymore. But all the Oak Park damsels are going to have to show something. I'm off of them the whole bunch. . . . The Doc says I'm all shot to pieces, figuratively as well as literally."

Hemingway's experience in WWI provided the backdrop for his 1929 masterpiece, *A Farewell to Arms*, and von Kurowsky became the model for doomed nurse Catherine Barkley.

After 1918, all references to Annette in his writing disappeared. Annette herself seems to evaporate from history, not even appearing in Oak Park's 1918 high school yearbook. Today, there are no DeVoes left in Oak Park.

After hitting a few dead ends, I stumbled across an entry in the 1921 Harvard Alumni Bulletin announcing the "engagement of C. George Krogness Jr., to Miss Annette DeVoe . . . 23 of Oak Park, Ill."

Annette Krogness died on October 16, 1982, and was buried in Cleveland's Lake View Cemetery.

Searching for relatives in Ohio, I spoke with Annette's son, John Krogness.

Yes, he said, "Mom dated Hemingway briefly," but he didn't have any other details, just that "they went to the movies together." He remembers his father talking about attending English class with Hemingway, who turned in a jungle story in which the hero gets captured by natives who "sandpapered his eyeballs."

He describes his mother as "outspoken," "very elegant," and "a homemaker all her life." She was a very accomplished floral arranger, he added.

This single phone call turned into a flurry of Krogness family correspondence. When Annette's granddaughter, Sarah Godfrey, hears Hemingway's opening line about her grandmother's "grace" and "sensuous loveliness," it spurs an immediate reaction.

"That sounds like her . . . like how someone would describe her. She was very lovely, charming," Godfrey said.

Annette's grandson John Godfrey remembers reading Hemingway's books in high school and being told, "Your grandma used to go out with him."

When he asked his grandmother about it, Annette said, "Oh, yeah. He's kind of a kook."

"She didn't want to talk about it and was just trying to get past it," he said.

Among Annette's three children and three grandchildren, there's debate about what kind of relationship she had with Hemingway. It stems, in part, from the fact that any teenage romance with Hemingway would be counter to the family narrative.

Annette met her future husband, George Krogness, when she was fourteen and he attended Oak Park and River Forest High School as a freshman.

"The family story is that they met and she fell in love with my grandfather at a very young age," Godfrey said. "They had a wonderful romance and marriage. There would have never been any discussion about her with anyone else."

Enter the young Hemingway, then known to his classmates as "Ernie," the handsome aspiring writer who played almost all the high school sports but excelled at none of them. When Ernie and Annette knew one another, George was attending Chicago's Latin School and, later, Phillips Exeter Academy in New Hampshire.

Sarah Godfrey thinks it's possible that her grandmother and Hemingway "had a little teenage romance going on . . . but you wouldn't have heard about it. She never talked about it, and that was entirely in character for her."

She adds: "I can completely see how he could be infatuated with her. Whether anything was reciprocated, it's very hard to say."

Annette didn't graduate with her 1918 senior class. She was sent off to boarding school in Massachusetts—possibly because of her mother's ill health—and then attended Smith College.

What impact Annette had on Hemingway's life is uncertain, but in the author's novels and his life, love was an elusive thing. Though there's passion and romance in his work and letters, love was often hindered by impassable obstacles (age, injury, timing). Hemingway was shattered when von Kurowsky left him for an engagement to an Italian officer. Afterward the author tended to leave his romantic partners before they left him, or he would passive-aggressively force a breakup. Hemingway was a writer in love with love but mystified by the fundamentals that gave it longevity.

In the map of the author's romantic life, this pencil-scribbled discovery represents the beginning: Hemingway's first-known love poem. Von Kurowsky burned all of her love letters from him, and most of the letters to his first wife, Hadley Richardson, didn't survive. It's a rare find, according to Hemingway biographer Scott Donaldson, author of *By Force of Will: The Life and Art of Ernest Hemingway*.

"Once in a great while these discoveries come to light. And sometimes, as in this case, they tell us something absolutely new about their subject," he wrote in an email. "This comes as a surprise, and a welcome one, showing that young Hemingway was as susceptible as most other youths to developing ardent, if temporary, feelings for members of the opposite sex. . . . The standard biographies portray him as for the most part uninterested in girls."

Annette's family is surprised, too. Sadly, however, no one in the family can find any of Annette's correspondence, from Hemingway or anyone else. Even a family history, written by her husband, reveals few details. He wrote, "My deepest satisfactions are in having known Annette since I was fifteen, in having been married to her for 47 years, and in seeing our children become damn fine people."

Annette's middle grandchild, Kate Dwyer, keeps a snapshot that Hemingway gave to her grandmother on a table in her living room. In it, Hemingway stands alone, dressed in an Italian officer's uniform and cape, leaning on a cane. The inscription on the back, in the author's handwriting, reads: "Tenente Ernest M Hemingway 1919." (*Tenente* is Italian for "lieutenant"; Hemingway was a second lieutenant, or *sottotenente*, in the Red Cross.)

Dwyer, sixty-one, keeps the snapshot in her living room next to a photo of her father.

"The pictures look good together," and they make an interesting conversation piece, she said.

When asked why the photo was kept by three generations of her family, she stops to think.

"Either she had some connection to him and never spoke of it, or she kept it and he turned out to be the most famous man in America," Dwyer said.

"I always thought she must have had an adventurous streak hiding under those layers of decorum," she continues. "But sadly, I was too young to understand or explore this part of my grandmother's personality and history. I wish I had."

Kathryn Longwell

She was just Hemingway's type: a beautiful singer with a stunning, sultry voice.

So when the nineteen-year-old Hemingway returned home from World War I with a broken heart and a limp, it was Kathryn Longwell that he took on romantic canoe trips along the Des Plaines River.

"We'd paddle for miles," she told Hemingway's younger brother, Leicester, years later, "and other times we would come to my home and read stories he had written, while eating little Italian cakes that he brought from the city."

Longwell was a transitional figure in Hemingway's romantic life and the audience for some of his earliest short stories. Yet, Longwell receives only a few sentences in Hemingway biographies, when she shows up at all. Hemingway was so taken with her that he gave her his Italian officer's cloak—a gesture that so enraged Hemingway's mother that she demanded its return.

No photos of Longwell appear in Hemingway's yearbooks, because she was two years younger than he was at Oak Park River Forest High School. Even fewer stories survive.

But who was Kathryn Longwell?

Both Hemingway and Longwell attended OPRF High School, although they didn't seem to overlap much in their extracurricular lives. She was her class vice president and participated in no fewer than nine activities, including opera, French Club, Drama Club, and the Girls' Rifle Club.

Whatever their connection, Hemingway wrote Longwell a postcard in April 1919, after he recovered from shrapnel wounds he sustained while serving in the American Red Cross.

It was while he was convalescing in Italy that Hemingway fell in love with Agnes von Kurowsky. Only a few weeks after his return to Oak Park from Italy, however, von Kurowsky called off their romance, and Hemingway didn't wait long before trying to mend his broken heart by dating Longwell.

The early stories he read to her could have been drafts of "The Mercenaries," "Cross Roads" and "The Current"—stories in which Hemingway was already exploring themes that would resonate throughout his career: betrayal, personal morality, and the cost of violence.

Some sleuthing at the Oak Park History Museum and the University of Chicago archives helped me find her son, Peter Davis.

"My mother was rather close-lipped" about Hemingway, Davis remembered. Davis thought that after an embarrassed Hemingway retrieved his Italian cloak at the insistence of his mother in 1919, he might have given Longwell one of his war medals instead. But if there was a medal or other correspondence between them, the items were lost.

Only fragments of family stories survive, including the time when Davis's father, Howard Grenville Davis, was still courting Longwell and visited her home.

"On the piano was a picture of Ernest Hemingway," Davis said.

If his father saw Hemingway as any sort of rival, however, the elder Davis prevailed when he married Longwell in 1927, after she graduated with a degree in philosophy from the University of Chicago.

Newspapers and yearbooks from the 1920s portray Longwell as a popular chanteuse. In 1921, she performed in "The Joy of Singhai" at the University of Chicago's Mandel Hall.

The college newspaper, the *Daily Maroon*, praised Longwell, writing that she "sang the best of the evening's music in the best of the evening's voices" when she performed "Chinatown Blues" and "Cherry Blossom Bungalow."

In college, Longwell lettered in field hockey and was active in the Women's Athletic Association.

Longwell's niece, Mary Jean Stephen, remembers her "aunty" as "tall, with dark hair and very striking-looking. She was very forceful; she was not anyone who retreated to the background."

Stephen remembers her concise speech and that she was always dressed impeccably in handmade French fashions.

"Aunty had this very sultry singing voice in the style of a night-club singer. A beautiful, low voice," Stephen recalled.

Her husband, who went by his middle name, Grenville, served as his wife's accompanist on piano when they held soirees at their home. The couple lived in Oak Park, Riverside, and Winnetka before moving to North Carolina.

"They had wonderful parties and they were the entertainment," Stephen said. "You wouldn't miss one."

Kathryn and Grenville were business partners as well as musical ones. In 1936, they founded the Grenville Davis Company, a successful office products and commercial furniture business, which the family still runs today. Later in life, Kathryn was a dedicated hospital volunteer and died near Tryon, North Carolina, in 1974 after a shift at a local hospital.

It's unknown how much contact Longwell had with Hemingway after 1919, although Davis also remembers a visit to Cuba with his mother in the 1950s, "before Castro."

"I know my mother talked to [Hemingway] on the telephone," said Davis, but "we didn't get to meet him."

As for the reason Hemingway and Longwell broke up, that also remains a mystery, although it was likely because Hemingway traveled to Michigan in the summer of 1919 and the two simply went their separate ways.

Neither of his parents talked about Longwell's courtship with the budding author, Davis said.

"I'm glad she didn't marry Ernest Hemingway, believe me. What a crazy life."

Frances Coates

In 2017, Betsy Fermano walked through an exhibition titled "Ernest Hemingway: Between Two Wars" at the John F. Kennedy Library and Museum in Boston. Among the artifacts—vintage photos, paintings, and handwritten stories from Hemingway—she spotted a family name in a manuscript on display: Coates.

Frances Elizabeth Coates was Fermano's grandmother and Hemingway's high-school classmate. He used a version of her name— "Liz Coates"—in his sexually charged 1923 story "Up in Michigan." The name Frances also appears in two of his novels: *The Sun Also Rises* (1926) and *To Have and Have Not* (1937).

That's because Hemingway was infatuated with her. The two briefly dated, though almost no one knew of their history. For Fermano, a retired development executive, it wasn't a surprise: she had one-hundred-year-old letters from Hemingway that no one outside the family knew about.

In July 1918, a young Ernest Hemingway wrote, "I can't break the habit of writing you whenever I get a million miles away from Oak Park."

This early correspondence was a rare discovery.

"This is a really fascinating find," said Sandra Spanier, a professor of English at Pennsylvania State University and general editor of the Hemingway Letters Project. "To find early letters like that—that's extremely rare. It's a fresh view of him."

Spanier says the new letters bring Hemingway's World War I experience "to light very vividly" and show a seldom-seen side of the budding author, since little material survives from that period.

"You hear him being flirtatious and kind of bragging, the way a teenage boy would. He's trying to make her a little bit jealous," she says. "But he's also got this self-deprecating humor, which is quite charming. It's a completely different voice from others we've heard in his letters."

In 1918, not long after graduating high school, Hemingway headed to Italy to serve as a volunteer ambulance driver in World War I. After he was wounded by mortar fire, he spent some time in a Milan hospital, during which his mind returned to Coates.

The nineteen-year-old Hemingway remained so enamored of his former classmate that he wrote to his sister Marcelline, asking her to "call up Frances Coates and tell her that your brother is at death's door. And that will she please, no excuses, write to him. Make her repeat the address after so that she will have no alibi. Tell her that I love her or any damn thing."

Coates did write him back, although that letter is lost. What survived are two previously unknown letters from Hemingway to Coates, kept in a trunk for decades. The correspondence dates to a time when Hemingway was not yet famous—he had only a handful of short stories to his name.

In one of the letters, dated October 15, 1918, Hemingway writes on American Red Cross stationery, on the back of a hospital supper tray, "by the light of a candle stuck in a bayonet." He goes on: "I can now read, speak and write love letters in Italian. . . . I never cared to bring myself to address anyone as 'My treasure' but a 'Tesor a mea' [*sic*] just runs out of the pen. . . . Tis indeed a noble language and I'll have to haunt the fruit stands in the States to find somebody to work it off on!"

If the implication was that Frances could be that somebody, she did not appear to bite. And yet other items in Fermano's trunk show that she followed his life and career with interest. She held onto snapshots of a wounded Hemingway in Milan and some photos commemorating a canoe trip they took together. There's also an envelope of newspaper clippings that track Hemingway's rise to fame, chronicling his global adventures, his four marriages, and his suicide in 1961. Frances even kept Hemingway's high school photo in her dressing room, where it occupied a small gold frame, surrounded by gold lace. And Fermano held onto an unpublished, ten-page remembrance Frances wrote about growing up with "Ernie": a unique document that offers intimate insight into the author's teenage years in Oak Park, Illinois.

Reviewing Hemingway's letters from this period, I kept noticing Coates's name alongside DeVoe's. In fact, Hemingway's sister had needled him with a mocking sonnet about his crush on Coates, perhaps in retaliation for his penchant for opening her correspondence to "find out what the dames think of me."

"Frances his idol, with eyes of blue!" the poem begins:

> He wonders if F Coates is looking his way
> He straightens his tie, and heaves a great sigh
> But oh how he jumps to see when sweet F.C. comes by!
> No one likes Ernest, that is straight stuff
> And when he writes his stories we all say Enough

The poem reflects the popular opinion of the teenage Hemingway: even his high school friends said they were more likely to see him with a fishing rod than a girl. In 1984, more than six decades after he'd graduated from high school, his former classmate and neighbor Marian Kraft Larson told the *Chicago Tribune* that although Hemingway wasn't very "attractive to girls or with girls," he was "very popular with the boys."

Larson added, "Frances Coates was the only girl I remember seeing him with."

In our first phone call, I asked Fermano if she knew whether her grandmother dated Hemingway. Yes, Fermano said, she knew that Coates went out to dinner with the teenage Hemingway—but she suspected the interest was one-sided. In modern terms, Hemingway was stuck squarely in the friend zone.

"My grandmother always played it down, and they were always just friends," Fermano remembers. "There may or may not have been a possibility of that relationship developing, but, at the time, Frances was being courted by John Grace," a classmate she married in 1920.

Fermano knows this from bits of conversation from her very elegant but very private grandmother. She's also read Coates's then unpublished memories of the young Hemingway, which we've published in their entirety at the end of this book. Coates wrote that the teenage Hemingway was

a great, awkward boy falling over his long feet . . . in life, a disturbing person with very dark hair, very red lips. Very white teeth, very fair skin under which the blood seemed to race, emerging frequently in an all-enveloping blush. What a help his beard, later was to be, protecting and covering this sensitivity. The whole of his face fell apart when he laughed.

They had "lots of nice times," Coates wrote, "skating, walks, movies and opera."

Also in the document are descriptions of Hemingway's mother ("A big, majestic woman . . . [who] moved as a ship does, with great majesty and authority") and a biting assessment of Hemingway's personality ("The inferiority complex remained to the end and with it came the braggadocio and the need to become somebody to himself . . . a quick and deadly jealousy of his own prestige and a constant . . . and consuming need for applause").

Fermano never thought that anyone would want letters almost a century old that Hemingway had written to an unknown classmate. Coates and Hemingway shared proximity on the staff of their high school literary magazine, the *Tabula*, where Hemingway was a contributor and she was the music editor. She was a year older than him, a senior when he was a junior.

Coates herself was a discreet figure. Though she'd become a successful local opera singer who was used to being featured in the press, she didn't publicize her connection with Hemingway, and she was hesitant to talk about it—even when approached by the author's first biographer, Princeton University professor Carlos Baker, in 1963 and again in 1966. She was reluctant to add to the cult of Hemingway that had sprung up, and remembering those years in Oak Park was trying—Coates's mother was sick then, and had died young.

Baker does, however, mention Coates in a single, powerful paragraph that traces Hemingway's infatuation with her to an April 1916 performance of *Martha*, a three-act high school opera. On stage, Coates played a huntress in the chorus and "Third Servant." Baker writes, "Playing his cello in the orchestra pit, Ernest could hardly keep his eyes on the score. His friend Al Dungan, a gifted cartoonist, made a caricature of a boy with desperate eyes and labeled it: 'Erney sees a girl named Frances.' He was too shy to ask her to the Junior-Senior prom on May 19."

In an undated, unsent letter written after the book's publication, Coates thanks Baker for an insight: "I never understood, until reading your book, [Hemingway's] bitter remark when I told him John and I were engaged: 'All the good girls are taken!'"

Two decades later, Hemingway may have aired some of his bitterness in *To Have and Have Not*. Reading the novel, Frances recognized broad caricatures of herself and John, who attended the University of Wisconsin and became a successful railroad executive—especially when Hemingway tells of a young man sworn into an elite, Ivy League secret society:

The fiancé is a Skull and Bones man, voted most likely to succeed, voted most popular, who still thinks more of others than of himself and would be too good for anyone except a lovely girl like Frances. He is probably a little too good for Frances too, but it will be years before Frances realizes this, perhaps; and she may never realize it, with luck. The type of man who is tapped for Bones is rarely also tapped for bed; but with a lovely girl like Frances intention counts as much as performance.

Coates couldn't miss the note of resentment in it: "I went to the Country Club dances with John, rode in his father's high and shiny Packard car, as I realize how it must have seemed to Ernie (one doesn't sense those things when one is young)."

Hemingway's mother seems to have admired Coates as much as he did. In her family scrapbook, Mrs. Hemingway underlined Coates's name in the program from the opera where she first caught the young Hemingway's eye. Next to it, she wrote: "The most graceful, dainty and charming girl on the High School stage. She is adorable."

At least one letter from Coates to Mrs. Hemingway survives in the Harry Ransom Center in Austin. In May 1924, Coates writes, "The gift of your friendship and sympathy is one that I have treasured thru the years."

Coates's documents pose a few new mysteries. She references other letters that Hemingway wrote her from Kansas City, where he worked as a reporter for the *Kansas City Star* before he volunteered for the Red Cross. That correspondence has never been recovered—nor has a letter to Coates from his sister Marcelline, in which she blames

Frances for her brother's running off to volunteer for the American Red Cross. If Coates had returned his affection, Marcelline implies, Hemingway might have seen fit to stay put.

Marcelline was working the other side, too: she never discouraged Hemingway from pining for Coates, even after her engagement. In a letter dated July 5, 1918, Marcelline wrote to him in Italy: "I suppose you heard . . . Frances Coates & Jack Grace are engaged? It was announced the day after you left! (Wise Frances!)" The next month, on August 25, she added: "In my previous letters I told you about Frances Coates' engagement to Jack Grace, but I'll tell her to write you anyway. She isn't wedded yet, y'know."

As for Hemingway and Coates themselves, the last surviving letter between them was from Coates, in January 1927, when Hemingway's first son, John, was three, and—unbeknown to Coates—his marriage to his first wife, Hadley, had broken down.

"I just finished *The Sun Also Rises* and you are before me so vividly that I must tell you how much I enjoyed the book," she writes, calling the novel "heartbreaking." She continues: "The years are making you a strange person—I should so love to see you—I haven't seen Marce for over a year—but someone said you were returning. I have a ravishingly beautiful daughter to match your son—and I'd so like meeting your nice Hadley. . . . Jack joins me and wanting to see you both."

Fermano doesn't know if Hemingway responded, or if they ever saw each other again.

Her grandmother, despite the nostalgia that comes with such keepsakes, was clearly happy with her choice. Frances and John were married for sixty-seven years. They raised a daughter, traveled the world, and died a year apart, in 1988 and 1989. On the front of the envelope containing her photos with Hemingway, Coates wrote, "Ernie Pictures / And 25 years later ooh! Am I glad I married John."

On the next few pages, we've printed Coates's original description of what it was like growing up with a teenage Ernest Hemingway.

Growing Up with Ernest Hemingway

Foreword by Robert K. Elder

Frances Coates's ten-page remembrance about growing up with Ernest Hemingway, along with the photographs and Hemingway's letters, was sold on December 11, 2017, to an unknown buyer for $20,000. Coates's granddaughter, Betsy Fermano, retained the copyright on her grandmother's writing, however, and was gracious enough to allow us to publish it here, for future generations of Hemingway fans.

While Frances and Carlos Baker, Hemingway's first biographer, never met, they did correspond, and she answered a few of his questions. But ultimately Coates never granted Baker a full interview. In letters included in this lot, she apologized in the unsent letter and explains that she was reluctant to add to what she calls Hemingway's "I Knew Him When" cult in Oak Park. Remembering her time in high school was painful for Frances, because at the time her mother was dying after a long battle with cancer. It's unknown why she never sent the letter or the monograph to Baker, both of which were written after 1969. Her reluctance to contribute to Baker's biography could have been, in part, because while she was socializing with the teenage Hemingway, her declared boyfriend was away.

"She was very private about it. I think Ernie meant a lot to her and she was very protective of their relationship," says Fermano.

Here we've included her unsent letter to Baker, plus the full text of the remembrance.

I've written elsewhere, notably on the *Paris Review* website[27] and in Northwestern University's alumni magazine,[28] about Frances's life and her impact on Hemingway. But here, Frances's own charming account of their relationship provides significant insight into the life of the young writer. What I love most about the essay is Coates's view into Hemingway's psyche and family life.

In editing this piece for publication, I've left intact her flowery, extravagant prose. I've corrected a few titles and dates, and added annotations for a modern reader.

After the original stories ran, I found recordings of Frances's singing. It was her voice that made Hemingway fall in love with her, as he listened to Frances perform in *Martha*, their high school opera. He was in the orchestra pit, playing cello.

I also uncovered correspondence that Frances wrote to Hemingway's mother in 1924 and, in the forthcoming essay, she mentions Madelaine "Sunny" Hemingway's trips to Ernest's home in Cuba—evidence that Frances's relationship with the family went well beyond high school.

As I was preparing this manuscript, Fermano found her grandmother's baby book, which included an invitation to the baby shower of Hemingway's sister, Marcelline. There is plenty more for future scholars to uncover about the connection between these two families.

Robert K. Elder
Oak Park, Illinois
January 2023

Frances Coates's Unsent
Letter to Carlos Baker

Dear Mr. Baker,

I am most remiss in writing you to thank you for putting me so nicely in your book about Ernest Hemingway. I feel very sorry about this and hope you will forgive my silence. I have started many times to write you but somehow it was most difficult because it touched a part of my youth that set off an almost endless train of poignant memories, not of Ernie, but of my mother.[29] I have re-evaluated my whole life and, now that I am a mother and a grandmother, I question myself anew and hope that I have become the person she so wished.

I very much enjoyed your book, quite apart from its subject. The style is so limpid, the understanding so gentle, the humor so kindly and the analysis so deadly correct. And when you were interviewed here by Robert Cromie[30] your presence confirmed it all: Would that all biographies could be so well done!

No, I wasn't the girl to whom Ernie gave his Italian uniform cape, to which his mother took umbrage. She would have given me the cape and the boy too, and to her last days she would remember those early days. Young people can be very cruel and draw fine lines between "groups" that seem absurd in later years. . . . And Ernie and "Marce" were a bit "different."

I read your book with an echo forever following. The events in Ernie's life came back to us at the time in Oak Park as acts in a play: unreal, far away, and mostly un-understandable. "Two wives living around the corner from each there in Paris, baby-sitting with each other's small sons?" Strange. And we felt comforted that our own small daughter still had the same parents she started out with. "Ernie had become a Catholic?" He had always wanted to "belong" and this was it, perhaps. That chap in *The Sun Also Rises* . . . sad, but why go on about it? I knew about Lady Brett, too. She, too, was one rung up Ernie's social ladder! We stopped playing bridge and over our tea wondered how the Hemingway's breezy, late-afternoon porch would look to Maria when Robert Jordan sent her "home to his mother" in *For Whom the Bell Tolls.* Sunny's visits to the Finca in Cuba and to Key West were hilarious. It was nice, after the house on Kenilworth was sold, to hear he had bought the house on Key-stone Avenue in River Forest for his mother, but no one wanted to see him when he was there . . . and I doubt that he wanted to see us: Fame, however heady, could never compensate or change an eternal inferiority complex. Later, of course, they capitalized on him. The "I Knew Him When" cult came into being, not only his family, who had a heyday, but classmates and remote, erstwhile associates. Success, however, varnishes every early opinion, and most of us were glad for Ernie.

Your Mr. Waring Jones[31] was most courteous and thoughtful and interested. I should be most grateful if you would beg his forgiveness, too, for me! And I am forever in your debt.

I don't know quite why I sent you the enclosed monograph. Could you return it? It is largely because your inquiries started this train of memories. I could have added little to your excellent story, except in the late winter and spring of 1919 when Ernie returned from Italy. I have a fine snapshot of the tall figure, overseas cap at a jaunty angle, full-circle black cape a-fling, cane, and booted legs toe-ing inwards in typically awkward pose. He came often to my mother's house and I was part of the parties given by the Italians, the first one instigated by the fruit storeowners of Forest Park, later attracting the Chicago group. We had many happy times together and with Marce. I heard briefly about the little Italian nurse, only she was a Contessa in whose home he convalesced, but I never understood, until reading your book, his bitter remark when I told him John and I were engaged: "All the good girls are taken!"

So, I thank you again for your beautifully written book for your interest, which sent me down the fresh, green springtime path of my youth.

Sincerely,
Frances Grace

Remembering Hemingway

Frances Coates Grace

Really I wish I might tell you how fresh and green it is still, the first time Ernie swam into my vision. The tender green of youth and growing things, our time of life perhaps (we were sixteen, I a few months older); the time of year—it was spring; the soft green of early twilight on the river grand, the shimmering green of tree-reflecting water, as the canoe glided along, everything rich and soft and flowing, glissando, waiting in that magic moment, suspended, before settling into a mold. A most hopeful time, kind and shy, waiting to bloom. Whatever comes later, one is grateful for remembered beginnings.

Ernie has asked me to go up the river ("the raging Des Plaines") for a picnic supper cooked over a fire, with his sister Marcelline and her beau, Harold Sampson. Dr. Hemingway, having brought us out in his busily energetic car, leaned over the bridge railing above to wave us on our way. The crepuscule[32] envelopes the picture as a fixative in my mind.

It was really quite a thing for Ernie to do. His bravery was a surprise to me. Oak Park High was a big school. There were many cliques (young people are cruel) and ours had never coincided. My kind of heart has always betrayed me and perhaps I wanted to put him at ease.

But there he was, a great, awkward boy falling over his long feet, moving slowly, inclusively, a trifle bent over as though to examine things more closely (immensely tall Henry Beston, did the same thing later because of his deafness and I'm 5'2"), his arms wide to include all men, all experiences, or to balance his awkwardness . . .

—in life, a disturbing person with very dark hair, very red lips, very white teeth, very fair skin under which the blood seemed to race, emerging frequently in all-enveloping blush. What a help his beard, later was to be, protecting and covering this sensitivity. The whole of his face fell apart when he laughed. There were dimples, a wide grin and a suave and pleasing voice, like Marce's, a legacy no doubt from their singing mother.

And everyone knew the Hemingways—a big family in a big house on north Kenilworth Avenue distinguished by an enormous room to the north, a "studio" where Mrs. Hemingway held "musicales." A big, majestic woman, a singer in her youth naturally a contralto, she moved as a ship does, with great majesty and authority. She must sometimes have worn dresses other than long, but I can never remember her in anything but long, black, trailing dresses and pearls reflecting her white hair, spectacles mirroring her placidity. She would descend on us, over a puzzle or games, to announce pontifically, "If you will come to my room at three o'clock, I should like to read to you." And we appeared dutifully, were read to and dismissed, after a time, meek and quiet. (At 60 or 65 she took up painting, lots of "dunes" pictures, and was quite successful at selling them.)

One sensed the rigid discipline of the household, here. One never danced at the Hemingways'. At other houses the rugs were rolled back and the Victrola happily wound up, but on great occasions, invitations arrived from Ernie and Marcelline with "'Salmagundi'" (whatever that was!)[33] in the lower left-hand corner. We thought it quaint, but I always enjoyed it, as I did all the other times in that house. There was much banter and humour among the children, Marcelline, Ernie, Ursula, Leicester, and "Sunny" and always a baby; the wit flying back and forth, everyone with those wide, sweet mouths, in constant laughter, cloaking everyday thoughts in dramatic, extravagant language.

If Mrs. Hemingway were austere, it was Dr. Hemingway who warms me most. Ernie, later, was the exact image of his father, with a few more whispers. A doctor of medicine, he was forever popping back home between calls and inhabiting a small room at the front of the house, an office of sorts, genial, interested, kind and generous. His family home was over on Oak Park Avenue, his own father was at that time still alive and Miss Grace, the doctor's sister, was a gracious and charming lady, pretty. Later she married and lived in Honolulu.

Ernie adored his father and was proud of the things he learned from him. At the family's summer cottage at Walloon Lake in northern Michigan, they must have loved being together, finding the intimate ways of nature, hunting, fishing, and exploring that follow in all Ernie's writing. When we passed the game preserve on the River Road just below the new country club, Ernie would point out the low-flying pheasant, the scuttling chipmunk, and the wedge of duck overhead. I remembered this early love in the dreadful *Across the River and into the Trees*[34] which, otherwise, was so filled with vindictive hatred of his third wife, or fatuous disdain for the military. Ernie himself knew how bad this book was for he set about immediately to vindicate himself and earn eternal vindication and the world-wide gratitude for "The Old Man and the Sea" plus the Nobel Prize.

I seem to remember this Hemingway household warmly, even though it was not my world exactly. While my own home was modest and my mother sad and ill, there was an echo here at the Hemingways' of my little-girlhood when my much older brothers and sisters filled our home with activity, albeit a bit more worldly. The house of my John,[35] who even then was tucked in the back of my mind and heart as the Beginning and End of all things for me, was most conventional, conservative and austere, so that this warmth pleased me. I went to the Country Club dances with John, rode in his father's high and shiny Packard car, as I realize now it must have seemed to Ernie (one doesn't sense those things when one is young). It is in *To Have and to Have Not*, I think, that there is a girl with my name, whose fiancé is sarcastically "tapped" on the shoulder for membership in a stratum of life unattainable to the writer and the hero. It is a wry scene.[36]

Ernie's first stories which appeared in the High School "Tabula" and "Trapeze" were patterned on Ring Lardner's[37] epics appearing in the Chicago Tribune and I thought them immeasurably stupid. Why anyone would go to the trouble to try to talk like that or, worse, to copy it, was beyond me. Miss Dixon, our English teacher, took us all over to the University of Chicago to take the Scholarship Exams, and most of us were enamored of sweeter sounding phrases, a more elegant style. Who could foresee the spectre of realism waiting to engulf the whole world or the arts, the black stream of crudity and indecency that has submerged us, or that Ernie would be in its vanguard? Ring Lardner indeed! To me, at sixteen, football players were, and still are the epitome of stupidity. Their heads were so hard there was no room for brains and their extreme and oafish activity put them to sleep at parties, mercifully for me. Now swimming, I would argue (my John was on his university swimming team), tennis, riding (my husband still keeps his horses), skating, golf, shooting-games that take real skill—were a different matter enlisted my respect. Sportsmanship should be of a higher order, involving technique and all it implies. I seem to sense this involvement with skill and the appreciation of style years later in the marvelous ballet of bull-fighting in *Death in the Afternoon*, and interested always, in guns and the skill of hunting.

At the end of my Freshman year in college, I began to study music seriously and, my lovely mother being sad and ill, I stayed at home in Oak Park. There were letters from Ernie in Kansas City[38] where he had gone to learn to be a journalist and to stay with his uncle. Then Toronto where he cubbed on the Star. Then from Italy where he went to cover the war and joined the Italian Ambulance Corps.[39] I wish I had kept them all, but these few are interesting enough. One can trace the experiences and places in *A Farewell to Arms*. Catherine and the little contessa Ernie wrote about to me are very much alike. And the grouse-hunting in my letter is surely part of the dreadful *Across the River and into the Trees* countryside, the Abruzzi, etc.

Ernie came home on convalescent leave in the late winter and early spring of 1919. See the picture of him in front of our house on Pleasant Street in Oak Park.[40] Note the bravado angle of the kepi,[41] the uniform cut like a civilized jacket (our U.S. boys, as you remember, were all done up in band masters' outfits: braid straight up the front to the still, uncompromising collar designed to keep the chin up and no mistake, their legs wound in endless puttees).

Note Ernie's Italian uniform with proper lapels, like the British the long, soft boots; and over all, the swashbuckling, full-circle black cape! And the wide, crimson and white grin! The Nineteenth Century Woman's Club[42] had never seen the like of it and listened enraptured, to "War Experiences." Madame Mare[43] enjoyed it pontifically and the good doctor was quiet and moist-eyed.

The Italians of Chicago and Oak Park and its environs were wonderful! Ernie was the first American wounded in Italy and soon he was home. The party described in the article[44] was something I shall always treasure. The world was almost young, we were to save it, remember, and many people believed that Mr. Wilson[45] could bring out the latent qualities of good will in every nation. The local Italian colony came to serenade Ernie one night and I happened to be there for supper. A proper leader introduced himself and Ernie spoke to them in Italian, leaning over the porch railing. From the shadows they emerged, the fruit vendors of Forest Park and the West Side, their faces shining in the light of the porch lamps. Someone had a hurdy-gurdy and there were presents of fruit and wine, and a proper speech. Ernie thanked them modestly in, to our ears, marvelously fluent Italian. A week later there was a dinner at the Hemingways' but brought in by the guests and complete in every detail. Food, wine, and delicious "dolces," cooked and served by the guests. The opera singer spoken of in the article was from the Civic Opera and, finding no one able to accompany him, stood at the piano, one foot on the pedal, occasionally striking a vague chord, but singing ecstatically his face illumined, his audience enraptured. The Old World thanked the New in grateful, unmistakably romantic accents in unromantic Chicago!

Going to the theatre was an adventure, too. Ernie's "bad" leg was stiff, so we had aisle seats in order to keep it out straight. The "different," distinguished uniform and a touch of ham in its wearer, delighted everyone and invited comment. One night we supped afterward at the old Terrace Garden. The couple one tier above us, middle-aged, nice-looking people, watched us carefully and, as they left, dropped a folded note on the table.

Ernie flushed and started after them, but decided to read the note[46] first. Such nice young people we must have been and the couple, visiting from England, thought so too! As similar incident is in one of his stories,[47] only the note was an insult and an equivalent to an invitation to a duel. And naïve we were, too. I remember trying valiantly to smoke a cigarette, with Marcelline cheering, coughing myself into a frenzy amid swirls of smoke. Nowadays, you can't qualify as a teenager if you can't pack your liquor and your marijuana along with your switch blade! But then it was daring.

There were lots of nice times, skating, walks, movies, and opera. After-dinner coffee served in my mother's living-room was a pleasant novelty to Ernie and my concerts and musical interests were interesting to him. He was nice about my budding recognition.

But our paths were slowly separating, not that they had ever been very close. My responsibilities were increasingly heavy and when my mother died the next year, I was forever glad that I attended her so closely and lovingly. Then, too, as sailors do, my John came home from Officers' Training School, stumbling over his new sword, sporting, too, a full-circle, black broadcloth officer's cape! A familiar and beloved figure who sensed and shared my sadness and burdens too great for youth. Our engagement was announced that Christmas, and now, years later, I can still feel the glow and peace of that special Christmas-time.

And Ernie must have become part of the Chicago of that time, the early Twenties, a fabled time when our city was a Mecca for young and the not-so-young of the arts. One caught reverberations of it in going to lessons in the Fine Arts Building for years after. A special aura always surrounded that building. Scales and crescendos echoed in the halls. The Cordon Club, feminine counterpart of the very masculine Cliff Dwellers high in their eyrie[48] a block north, was in its heyday, presenting Mary Cameron's clever parodies on opera, etc., to standing ovations. I got to sing in "Hi Eda" and it was hilarious. Maurice Browne's Chicago Little Theatre, the first of its kind in America, flourished and the whole top floor was artists' studios. Ernest Klempner,[49] from Vienna, painted me in a pink "Manon"[50] costume and it was he who said, with his inimitable accent, "It is bewildering; in Europe we say we are a painter." In America they say, "I am an artist."

The huge portrait of Maggie Teyte[51] on the west wall of the stairwell on the sixth floor epitomizes the period: dim, romantic, idealistic, pretty. She smiled a bit mistily, a bit wryly when I spoke of it to her, years later. Yvette Guilbert[52] came to town, the respectability of delectable French dolkaonfa[53] taking the place of her naughty, long black gloves painted by Toulouse-Lautrec[54] in the Moulin Rouge posters. We had fine theatre concerts and opera, unhindered by the powerful and shameful unions of today. Dr. Stock,[55] urbane and frock-coated, continued Theodore Thomas'[56] great discipline of the Chicago Symphony Orchestra at Orchestra Hall where we strolled at intermission time, overlooking the Boulevard with the Lake[57] in the distance, and then repaired upstairs to tea at the Cliff Dwellers at concerts and to toast our toes at their fire and meet the artists. Opera, too. Campanini[58] and his great company at the Auditorium;[59] Mary Garden[60] and the unforgettable Pelleas[61] of Léon Rothier.[62] Her directorship of the Civic Opera was to come several years later. Ben Hecht[63] was even then rearing the brutal head of realism with Charles MacArthur, a brave but breathless second. Sherwood Anderson[64] (later to be felled by Ernie's criticism), his Ohio washing machine salesman days behind him, was trying to remember his early life. Thornton Wilder[65] came to teach at the University of Chicago and his "Cabala" followed.

And the young Hemingway must have moved among them, hesitant shy, belligerent, questing, overbearing, anxious, and kind. But not for long did he tarry.

We, John Grace and I, were married in 1920 and lived in a charming, tiny white gardener's cottage on Bonnie Brae Place approached by a path overhung with grape vines. Tiny, but with an enormous lot above where, among other festivities, we gave a party for Marceline and Sterling Sanford before their marriage. So we heard about Ernie's marriage to Hadley Richardson and wished him well. And soon afterward, they had left the Chicago scene; Ernie and Hadley, that sweet, good young woman, that stalwart soul, and set about partaking of their own Movable Feast on Paris' Left Bank. Hesitant, questing, watching; wrestling with the great truths within him to stew them out to the bewildered world; incorrigibly idealistic and romantic; going through, again, and again, one experience after another to find the core: marriage, many times, friendship and hero worship betrayed, religion from the fundamentalism of his youth through the stark mysticism of Catholicism, ideologies exploded, wars' exhaustion.

Whatever happened later on in life, I suspect bravery to be the "mean." The breathless bravery of the first four-letter words against his puritanical up-bringing; bravery against hypocrisy early known in his time; bravery against pomposity, windy pride and false modesty; bravery against symbolism and ideology owning and destroying men's souls; bravery against physical pain. His beloved father, remember, died by his own hand, an example his son felt compelled to follow and welcomed, I'm sure.

This is the portrait of a young man I once knew.

What the intervening years developed in him is quite another story. The potentials were there when I knew him. The inferiority complex remained to the end and with it came the braggadocio and the need to become somebody to himself; imagination and a sense of drama in that he was always watching himself perform; an enormous capacity for receiving and reassuring injury to his ego; a quick and deadly jealousy of his own prestige and a constant and touching and consuming need for applause. But through and beyond and overall was a blinding talent and the greatest requisite of all: the determination and industry to develop the technique to use it.

I think Ernie came full circle. I saw him start. Miss Mary Hemingway received and comforted the final package. I thank her, now, for a piece of his youth and hope that sometime she saw lurking behind that harsh and bristly beard a wide crimson and white grin staccato with deep, deep dimples.

Acknowledgments

From Thomas Bevilacqua

First, I would like to thank Robert K. Elder for being an exemplary coeditor on *Mythbusting Hemingway*. It has been a wonderful and illuminating experience getting to know and work with Rob through this process.

I also would like to thank Mark Cirino for being one of the architects of this book and for suggestions of questions to be answered.

Suzanne del Gizzo and Carl Eby recommended me for this project, and their vote of confidence means a great deal to me.

Rick Rinehart and Felicity Tucker deserve profuse thanks and much applause for their support, editorial guidance, and *immense* patience with this project. I am also quite grateful for David Dutton for his help and excellent representation with *Mythbusting Hemingway*.

There are many members of the Hemingway scholarly community whom I would like to thank for encouraging me and bringing me into this world of Hemingway scholarship; they include Robert Trogdon, Sara Kosiba, Kirk Curnutt, Gail Sinclair, Ross Tangedal, Hilary Kovar Justice, Verna Kale, Steve Paul, Marc Seals, Nicole Camastra, Michael von Cannon, and Mike Roos (to name just a few). Special thanks to Carl Eby and Robert Trogdon for their editorial thoughts and feedback.

As I mentioned in my introductory essay, Barry Maine's class at Wake Forest University led me into the world of Hemingway studies, and thus I would like to thank him here for that experience. I'd also like to acknowledge some of the many teachers I've had who encouraged my love of literature and, especially, Hemingway: Dell Martin, Carol Chacon, Sam Baker, Martin Kevorkian, Timothy Parrish, S.E. Gontarski, Andrew Epstein, and Christina Parker-Flynn.

I would like to acknowledge my colleagues at the Maclay School, especially my English department chair (Lee Norment), English department colleagues (Jessica Kerner, Craig Beaven, Lauren Fantle, Deborah Mayer, Cailyn Callaway), and other teachers and administrators (Chris Day, Ariel Evans, Katie Walker, Katy Gimbel, Joseph McCann, Charles Beamer, Angela Croston), for their support and inspiration.

I would not have seen the finish line without the help of Virginia and Elizabeth Lewis. Thank you both for being there when I needed you the most and helping me to realize this project. I truly appreciate it so much.

Finally, I would like to acknowledge and thank my family—mother, father, stepparents, grandparents, siblings, aunts, uncles, and cousins—for being a constant source of support no matter what.

From Robert K. Elder

I couldn't have asked for a better writing partner than Thomas Bevilacqua, who has been a delight to work with and a diligent researcher. Thanks also to Robert Trogdon and Carl Eby for their detailed feedback and edits, as well to Mark Cirino who helped conceive this project.

Lastly, I owe a never-ending debt of gratitude to my wife, Betsy Edgerton, and our twins—Eva and Dylan—who supported me writing this book through thick and thin, including family vacations.

NOTES

1. Dearborn identifies Jack Dempsey's hesitancy to spar with Hemingway as the reason why Tunney did not seem eager to spar with Hemingway.

2. For more about this, please see the chapter titled "Did Hemingway Suffer a Gunshot Wound While Fishing on the *Pilar*?"

3. As Bruccoli notes in his biography of Fitzgerald, "there is no record that they talked" at that final encounter (421).

4. For more that pertains to this, please see the chapter titled "Was Hemingway *Very* Particular about Hair?"

5. You can find more about this aspect of Hemingway's life in the chapter titled "Was Hemingway *Very* Particular about Hair?"

6. For example, see the chapters titled "Did Hemingway Have an Affair with Josephine Baker?" "Did Ava Gardner Skinny-Dip in Hemingway's Pool, and Did He Threaten to Fire Anyone Who Drained the Water?" and "Was Hemingway Friends with Marlene Dietrich?"

7. This title, when translated into English, means "What does the homeland tell you?"

8. For more on this, see the chapter titled "Did Hemingway Meet Benito Mussolini?"

9. For more on this, please see the chapter titled "Did Fidel Castro Use *For Whom the Bell Tolls* as a Guerrilla War Manual?"

10. As Spanier notes, Hemingway's presence in that 1934 issue of *Vanity Fair* was in the form of a paper doll that mocked Hemingway's public persona as the consummate "man's man," with the author in a leopard-skin loincloth.

11. See the chapter titled, "Did Hemingway Kill 122 Nazis during World War II?" for more on this.

12. For more on this, see the chapter titled "Did Hemingway Fight in World War I?"

13. See the chapter titled "Did Hemingway's Mother Dress Him Like a Girl?" for more about this.

14. See the chapter titled "Did Hemingway's Mother Dress Him Like a Girl?"

15. For more on this topic, see the chapter titled "Were Hemingway and F. Scott Fitzgerald in Love with Each Other?"

16. For more on this, see the chapter titled "Did Hemingway Box with Heavyweight Champion Gene Tunney?"

17. For more on this, see the chapter titled "Did Hemingway Get in a Fight with Writer Wallace Stevens?"

18. Also see the chapter titled "Did Hemingway Attempt Suicide More Than Once?"

19. I intend no disrespect to Gloria by retaining in quoted material masculine pronouns and the name Gregory. Gloria lived publicly and within her family for over sixty years as Gregory, and some degree of flexibility with names and pronouns was part of her life story. It would be difficult, and somewhat misleading, to edit it out.

20. Dearborn's source for this contention is Philip Griffin's biography of Hemingway, *Along with Youth*. That book uses images and incidents from Hemingway's fictional writing as biographical facts regarding the author. Griffin uses the writing in *A Farewell to Arms* to provide evidence about what happened to Hemingway himself.

21. This seems to be the incident that Dearborn dates as having occurred on April 18, 1961.

22. For more on this, see the chapter titled "Did an Infatuation Inspire Hemingway to Write *The Old Man and the Sea*?"

23. For more on Hemingway's suicide, see the chapters titled "Did Hemingway's Suicide Inspire a Famous Spider-Man Story?" "Was Hemingway Investigated by the FBI?" "Did Hemingway Survive Multiple Plane Crashes?" "Was Hemingway's Death Accidental?" "Did Hemingway Commit Suicide by Putting a Shotgun to His Forehead?" and "Did Hemingway Have Clinical Depression and Suicidal Tendencies on Both Sides of His Family?"

24. Though, as Mary Dearborn observes, "there is no record Ernest pitched in" (2017, 541) to give money to Ruth upon their mother's death.

25. Paul Mariani's biography of Stevens describes that punch thrown by Stevens as "break[ing] his right fist in two places" (207).

26. For more on this, see the chapter titled "Did Hemingway's Suicide Inspire a Famous Spider-Man Story?"

27. Robert K. Elder, "To Have and Have Not," *Paris Review*, May 4, 2017, https://www.theparisreview.org/blog/2017/05/04/to-have-and-have-not.

28. Robert K. Elder, "To Have and Have Not," *Northwestern Magazine*, Winter 2017, http://www.northwestern.edu/magazine/winter2017/feature/to-have-and-have-not-ernest-hemingway-love-interest-frances-coates.html.

29. Frances's mother was dying of cancer, which was difficult for Frances to look back on.

30. War correspondent for the *Chicago Tribune*.

31. Waring Jones (1928–2008) was a Minneapolis-based theatrical producer, writer, and a collector of Hemingway artifacts whose collection is now housed in the Oak Park Public Library, as part of the Ernest Hemingway Foundation of Oak Park Archives.

32. "Twilight."

33. Frances spelled this originally as "salamagundi," but she likely meant "salmagundi." According to the online *Oxford Living Dictionary*, salmagundi is (1) "A dish of chopped meat, anchovies, eggs, onions, and seasoning" or (2) "a general mixture; a miscellaneous collection."

34. Frances disliked Hemingway's novel so much that she refers to it as *Over the River and through the Trees* throughout the piece.

35. John Grace, whom Frances Coates would marry.

36. The passage Frances references is this one: "The fiancé is a Skull and Bones man, voted most likely to succeed, voted most popular, who still thinks more of others than of himself and would be too good for anyone except a lovely girl like Frances. He is probably a little too good for Frances too, but it will be years before Frances realizes this, perhaps; and she may never realize it, with luck. The type of man who is tapped for Bones is rarely also tapped for bed; but with a lovely girl like Frances intention counts as much as performance."

37. Ringgold Wilmer "Ring" Lardner (1885–1933), Hemingway's early journalistic hero, best known for his sports columns and short stories.

38. Unfortunately, Frances didn't save any of these letters.

39. Frances misremembers this detail. Hemingway volunteered with the American Red Cross.

40. Frances misremembers this, even inscribes it incorrectly on the back of the photo she owned. This is the famous photo of the young Hemingway, dressed in boots, a cape and cane, taken outside his family home at 600 North Kenilworth Avenue, in Oak Park.

41. A round-top military cap with a visor, popularized by the French.

42. A social club in Oak Park of which Hemingway's mother was a member.

43. Hemingway's mother, Grace Hall Hemingway.

44. Frances is referencing one of two newspaper articles in which the young Hemingway was interviewed dockside upon his return to the United States in 1919. They are: "Has 227 Wounds, But Is Looking for a Job," *New York Sun* (January 22, 1919) or "Worst Shot-up Man in U.S. on Way Home," *Chicago American* (January 21, 1919).

45. US president Woodrow Wilson.

46. The note, which was included and sold with Frances's lot of papers in 2017, read, "I just want to tell you, you are the finest, really dear sweet looking girl I've seen in Chicago."

47. This might be "The Mercenaries," written in 1919. The fact that it was published posthumously in 1985, sheds doubt on this. Hemingway may have shown her the story, however, as they were both in Oak Park in 1919.

48. High nest.

49. Artist Ernest Klempner (1867–1941) settled in the Chicago suburbs and painted a beautiful portrait of Frances, which was on display in the Three Arts Club for decades before it was given back to the family.

50. Title character of the 1884 comic opera by Jules Massenet.

51. Maggie Teyte (1888–1976) was a famous operatic soprano from England.

52. Yvette Guilbert (1865–1944) was a well-known French cabaret singer and actress.

53. Reference unknown.

54. Henri de Toulouse-Lautrec (1864–1901), the famed French painter.

55. Frederick Stock (1872–1942) served as the director of the Chicago Symphony Orchestra for thirty-seven years.

56. Theodore Thomas (1835–1905) was the founder of the Chicago Symphony Orchestra, as well as its first music director.

57. Lake Michigan.

58. Italian conductor Cleofonte Campanini (1860–1919).

59. The Chicago Grand Opera Company played at Auditorium Theatre, and Campanini served as the company's first conductor.

60. Mary Garden (1874–1967), an operatic soprano from Scotland.

61. One of the title characters from *Pelléas et Mélisande*, a 1902 opera by Claude Debussy.

62. Léon Rothier (1874–1951) was a famous operatic bass from France.

63. Ben Hecht (1894–1964) was a screenwriter, journalist, novelist, and playwright best known for coauthoring (with Charles MacArthur) *The Front Page*, a Broadway sensation in 1928.

64. Sherwood Anderson (1876–1941) was a famous journalist, short story writer, and novelist who encouraged Hemingway to move to Paris and provided him with an introduction to Gertrude Stein. The pair later fell out after Hemingway published *The Torrents of Spring* (1926), a parody of Anderson's novel *Dark Laughter* (1925).

65. Thornton Wilder (1897–1975) was a novelist and playwright best known for his play *Our Town*. He won three Pulitzer Prizes in his lifetime.

Works Cited

Baker, Carlos. *Ernest Hemingway: A Life Story*. Collier, 1969.

Baker, Jean-Claude, and Chris Chase. *Josephine: The Hungry Heart*. Random House, 1993.

Bates, Stephen. "'Unpopularity Is the Least of My Worries': Captain R. W. Bates and Lieutenant E. M. Hemingway." *Hemingway Review* 29, no. 1 (Fall 2009): 46–60.

Beevor, Antony. *The Spanish Civil War*. Penguin, 2001.

Benson, Jackson J. "Ernest Hemingway: The Life as Fiction and the Fiction as Life." *American Literature* 61, no. 3 (1989): 345–58.

Berry, Jeff. *Beachbum Berry's Potions of the Caribbean*. Cocktail Kingdom, 2013.

Birnbaum, Sarah. "Hemingway's Love Letter to Marlene Dietrich Goes on the Auction Block." The World, April 19, 2017. https://theworld.org/stories/2017-04-18/hemingways-love-letter -marlene-dietrich-goes-auction-block.

Biskind, Peter. *Easy Riders, Raging Bulls: How the Sex-Drugs-and-Rock 'n' Roll Generation Saved Hollywood*. Simon and Schuster, 1998.

Blume, Lesley M. M. *Everybody Behaves Badly: The True Story behind Hemingway's Masterpiece* The Sun Also Rises. Houghton Mifflin Harcourt, 2016.

Brown, David S. *Paradise Lost: a Life of F. Scott Fitzgerald*. Belknap, 2017.

Bruccoli, Matthew. *Some Sort of Epic Grandeur: The Life of F. Scott Fitzgerald*. University of South Carolina Press, 2002.

Burwell, Rose Marie. *Hemingway: The Postwar Years and the Posthumous Novels*. Cambridge University Press, 1996.

Callaghan, Morley. *That Summer In Paris*. Exile Editions, 2002.

Castro, Fidel, and Ignacio Ramonet. *My Life: A Spoken Autobiography*. Translated by Andrew Hurley. Scribner, 2007.

Cavanaugh, Jack. *Tunney: Boxing's Brainiest Champ and His Upset of the Great Jack Dempsey*. Ballantine, 2006.

Chamberlin, Brewster. *The Hemingway Log: A Chronology of His Life and Times*. University Press of Kansas, 2015.

Christian, Timothy. *Hemingway's Widow: The Life and Legacy of Mary Welsh Hemingway*. Pegasus, 2022.

Cirino, Mark, and Robert K. Elder. "Was Ernest Hemingway the Original American Sniper?" *HuffPost*, September 6, 2016.

Curtis, Wayne. *And a Bottle of Rum: A History of the New World in Ten Cocktails*. Crown, 2018.

Dearborn, Mary. *Ernest Hemingway: A Biography*. Vintage, 2017.

Deibler, William E. "The Fishing Was Good Too: Cuban Writer Claims Torrid Love Affair with Jane Mason Drew Hemingway to Havana." In *Hemingway, Cuba, and the Cuban Works*, edited by Larry Grimes and Bickford Sylvester, 61–71. Kent State University Press, 2014.

Di Robilant, Andrea. *Autumn in Venice: Ernest Hemingway and His Last Muse*. Knopf, 2018.

Diliberto, Gioia. *Paris without End: The True Story of Hemingway's First Wife*. Harper, [1992] 2011.

Donaldson, Scott. *Fool for Love: F. Scott Fitzgerald*. University of Minnesota Press, 2012.

———. "Hemingway and Suicide." *Sewanee Review* 103, no. 2 (Spring 1995): 287–95.

———. *Hemingway vs. Fitzgerald: The Rise and Fall of a Literary Friendship*. Overlook Press, 1999.

Eakin, Hugh. "The Old Man and the Farm: The Long, Tumultuous Saga of Ernest Hemingway's Prized Miró Masterpiece." *Vanity Fair*, October 2018. https://www.vanityfair.com/style/2018/09/ernest-hemingway-joan-miro-the-farm-painting.

Eby, Carl. "'Come Back to the Beach Ag'in David Honey!': Hemingway's Fetishization of Race in *The Garden of Eden* Manuscripts." *Hemingway Review* 14, no. 2 (1995): 98–117.

———. *Hemingway's Fetishism: Psychoanalysis and the Mirror of Manhood*. SUNY Press, 1998.

Elder, Robert K. "Archives Uncover Story of Hemingway's Forgotten Girlfriend." *Wednesday Journal*, November 27, 2018.

———. "Did Ernest Hemingway Have an Affair with His Sister-in-Law?" *HuffPost*, April 18, 2017.

———. "Hemingway's First Love, Annette Devoe." *Chicago Tribune*, July 12, 2016.

———. "How Ernest Hemingway Provided Inspiration for the Darkest Spider Man Story: 'Kraven's Last Hunt.'" *The Comics Journal*, February 22, 2021.

———. "New Hemingway Family Letter Points to History of Depression." *Wednesday Journal*, March 6, 2018.

———. "The 'Wide Lawns' Myth: Ernest Hemingway in Oak Park." *Chicago Tribune*, July 17, 2014.

———. "To Have and Have Not: New Letters Shed Light on Hemingway's Unrequited Love and Early Life." *The Paris Review*, May 4, 2017.

Ellman, Richard. *James Joyce*. Oxford, [1959] 1982.

Farah, Andrew. *Hemingway's Brain*. University of South Carolina Press, 2017.

Feldman Andrew. *Ernesto: The Untold Story of Hemingway in Revolutionary Cuba*. Melville House, 2019.

———. "Leopoldina Rodríguez: Hemingway's Cuban Lover?" *Hemingway Review* 31, no. 1 (Fall 2011): 62–78.

Felten, Eric. "A Cuban Summer Cooler." *Wall Street Journal*, August 4, 2007. https://www.wsj.com/articles/SB118617226986287654.

Fishelov, David. "The Poetics of Six-Word Stories." *Narrative* 27, no. 1 (January 2019): 30–46.

Fitch, Noel Riley. *Sylvia Beach and the Lost Generation: A History of Literary Paris in the Twenties and Thirties*. Norton, 1983.

Fitzgerald, F. Scott. *A Life in Letters*. Edited by Matthew J. Bruccoli. Scribner, 1995.

Florczyk, Steven. *Hemingway, the Red Cross, and the Great War*. Kent State University Press, 2014.

"For Sale, Baby Shoes, Never Worn." Quote Investigator, January 28, 2013. https://quoteinvestigator.com/2013/01/28/baby-shoes.

Fuentes, Norberto. *Hemingway in Cuba*. Translated by Consuelo E. Corwin. Edited by Larry Alson. Lyle Stuart, 1984.

Gardner, Ava. *Ava: My Story*. Bantam, 1990.

Gear, Matthew Asprey. "Three Dangerous Summers: Orson Welles's Unrealized Hemingway Trilogy." *Hemingway Review* 40, no. 1 (Fall 2020): 4.

Gingrich, Arnold. "Scott, Ernest and Whoever." *Esquire*, December 1, 1966, 186–89, 322–25.

Glass, Loren. *Authors Inc.: Literary Celebrity in the Modern United States, 1880–1980*. New York University Press, 2004.

Greene, Philip. *To Have and Have Another: A Hemingway Cocktail Companion*. Perigee, 2012.

Griffin, Peter. *Along with Youth: Hemingway, The Early Years*. Oxford University Press, 1985.

Hamilton, Sharon. "Ernest Hemingway and the Black Sox Trial." *SABR Black Sox Scandal Research Committee Newsletter* 12, no. 2 (December 2020): 15–17.

Hawkins, Ruth. *Unbelievable Happiness and Final Sorrow: The Hemingway-Pfeiffer Marriage*. University of Arkansas Press, 2012.

Hays, Peter. *The Critical Reception of Hemingway's* The Sun Also Rises. Camden, 2011.

Hemingway, Carol. "907 Whitehead Street." In *Key West Hemingway: A Reassessment*, edited by Kirk Curnutt and Gail D. Sinclair, 28–43. University Press of Florida, 2009.

Hemingway, Ernest. *By-Line: Ernest Hemingway: Selected Articles and Dispatches of Four Decades*. Edited by William White. Scribner, 1967.

———. *A Farewell to Arms*. Scribner, [1929] 1995.

———. *For Whom the Bell Tolls.* Scribner. 1995.

———. "Foreword." In *Treasury for the Free World*, edited by Ben Raeburn, xii–xvi. Arco, 1946.

———. *The Garden of Eden.* Scribner's, 1986.

———. "Interview with George Plimpton." In *The* Paris Review *Interviews*, 1:34–61. Picador, 2006.

———. *Islands in the Stream.* Scribner's, 1970.

———. *The Letters of Ernest Hemingway, Volume 1: 1907–1922.* Edited by Sandra Spanier and Robert W. Trogdon. Cambridge University Press, 2011.

———. *The Letters of Ernest Hemingway, Volume 2: 1923–1925.* Edited by Sandra Spanier, Albert J. DeFazio III, and Robert W. Trogdon. Cambridge University Press, 2013.

———. *The Letters of Ernest Hemingway, Volume 3: 1926–1929.* Edited by Rena Sanderson, Sandra Spanier, and Robert W. Trogdon. Cambridge University Press, 2015.

———. *A Moveable Feast: The Restored Edition.* Edited by Seán Hemingway. Scribner, 2009.

———. *The Old Man and the Sea: The Hemingway Library Edition.* Edited by Seán Hemingway. Scribner's, 2020.

———. *The Only Thing That Counts: The Ernest Hemingway/Maxwell Perkins Correspondence, 1925–1947.* Edited by Matthew Bruccoli. Scribner, 1996.

———. *Selected Letters 1917–1961.* Edited by Carlos Baker. Scribner, 2003.

———. *The Short Stories.* Scribner's, 2003.

———. *The Sun Also Rises & Other Writings 1918–1926.* Edited by Robert W. Trogdon. Library of America, 2020.

Hemingway, G. *Papa: A Personal Memoir.* Houghton Mifflin, 1976.

Hemingway, John. *Strange Tribe: A Family Memoir.* Lyons, 2007.

Hemingway, Mary Welsh. *How It Was.* Knopf, 1976.

Hemingway, Patrick. *Dear Papa: The Letters of Patrick and Ernest Hemingway.* Scribner, 2022.

Hemingway, Valerie. *Running with the Bulls: My Years with the Hemingways*. Ballantine, 2005.

"Hemingway Dead of Shotgun Wound; Wife Says He Was Cleaning Weapon." *New York Times*, July 3, 1961. https://archive.nytimes .com/www.nytimes.com/books/99/07/04/specials/hemingway -obit.html.

"Hemingway House Becomes a Museum." *New York Times*, February 2, 1964. https://www.nytimes.com/1964/02/02/archives/ hemingway-house-becomes-a-museum.html.

Hendrickson, Paul. *Hemingway's Boat: Everything He Loved in Life, and Lost, 1934–1961*. Knopf, 2011.

Hotchner, A. E. "Hemingway, Hounded by the Feds." *New York Times*, July 1, 2011. https://www.nytimes.com/2011/07/02/opin- ion/02hotchner.html.

———. *Hemingway in Love: His Own Story*. St. Martin's Press, 2015.

———. *Papa Hemingway*. Bantam, 1966.

Hutchisson, James M. *Ernest Hemingway: A New Life*. Pennsylvania State University Press, 2016.

Joiner, James. "The Hidden World of the Typewriter." *The Atlantic*, September 11, 2013. https://www.theatlantic.com/technology/ archive/2013/09/the-hidden-world-of-the-typewriter/279523.

Jules-Rosette, Bennetta. *Josephine Baker in Art and Life: The Icon and the Image*. University of Illinois Press, 2007.

Justice, Hilary K. "Music at the Finca Vigía: A Preliminary Catalog of Hemingway's Audio Collection." *Hemingway Review* 25, no. 1 (Fall 2005): 96–108.

Kahn, Roger. *A Flame of Pure Fire: Jack Dempsey and the Roaring '20s*. Harper Perennial, 2000.

Kale, Verna. *Ernest Hemingway: Critical Lives*. Reaktion, 2016.

Keach, Stacy. "My Favorite Ways to Kick the Bucket." *New York Times*, November 27, 2013. https://www.nytimes.com/2013/ 12/01/theater/stacy-keach-recalls-his-own-favorite-death-scenes .html.

Kert, Bernice. *The Hemingway Women*. Norton, 1998.

Lewis, Damien. *Agent Josephine: American Beauty, French Hero, British Spy*. Public Affairs, 2022.

Ludington, Townsend. *John Dos Passos: A Twentieth-Century Odyssey*. Carroll and Graf, 1980.

Lyman, Rick. "Martha Gellhorn, Daring Writer, Dies at 89." *New York Times*, February 17, 1998. https://www.nytimes.com/1998/02/17/arts/martha-gellhorn-daring-writer-dies-at-89.html.

Lynn, Kenneth S. *Hemingway*. Harvard University Press, 1995.

Mandel, Miriam B. "From the Hemingway Letters Project behind the Scenes with Pauline Pfeiffer Hemingway and Jane Kendall Mason." *Hemingway Review* 40, no.1 (Fall 2020): 104–21.

Mariani, Paul. *The Whole Harmonium: The Life of Wallace Stevens*. Simon and Schuster, 2016.

Martens, David B. "An Interview with Gigi's All-Stars at Ernest Hemingway's Finca Vigía, San Francisco de Paula, Cuba, July 6, 2004." In *Hemingway, Cuba, and the Cuban Works*, edited by Larry Grimes and Bickford Sylvester, 30–39. Kent State University Press, 2014.

McIver, Stuart. *Hemingway's Key West*. Pineapple Press, 2002.

Mellow, James R. *Hemingway: A Life without Consequences*. Da Capo, 1993.

Meyers, Jeffrey. *Hemingway: A Biography*. Da Capo, 1985.

Moorehead, Caroline. *Gellhorn: A Twentieth-Century Life*. Holt, 2004.

Morris, James McGrath. *The Ambulance Drivers: Hemingway, Dos Passos, and a Friendship Made and Lost in War*. Da Capo, 2017.

Mort, Terry. *Hemingway at War: Ernest Hemingway's Adventures as a World War II Correspondent*. Pegasus, 2016.

Ondaatje, Christopher. *Hemingway in Africa: The Last Safari*. Overlook Press, 2003.

"Our Gardens and Grounds." The Hemingway Home and Museum, 2021. https://www.hemingwayhome.com/our-architecture.

Paul, Steve. *Hemingway at Eighteen: The Pivotal Year That Launched an American Legend*. Chicago Review Press, 2017.

———. "Quotation Controversy—Writing and Bleeding." *THR Blog*, Hemingway Foundation and Society, May 27, 2016. https://www.hemingwaysociety.org/quotation-controversy-writing-and-bleeding.

Perkins, Maxwell. "Ernest Hemingway." *Book-of-the-Month Club News* (October 1920): 4.

Plimpton, George. *Shadow Box: An Amateur in the Ring*. Little Brown, [1977] 2016.

Reynolds, Michael. *Hemingway: The Final Years*. Norton, 1999.

———. *Hemingway: The 1930s*. Norton, 1999.

———. *Hemingway: The Paris Years*. Norton, 1999.

———. *The Young Hemingway*. Norton, 1999.

Reynolds, Nicholas. *Writer, Sailor, Soldier, Spy: Ernest Hemingway's Secret Adventures, 1935–1961*. William Morrow, 2017.

Robinson, Joshua. "Memories of Playing on Papa Hemingway's Ball Field." *New York Times*, October 6, 2008. https://www.nytimes.com/2008/10/07/sports/baseball/07hemingway.html.

Rose, Phyllis. *Jazz Cleopatra: Josephine Baker in Her Time*. Vintage, 1991.

Ross, Lillian. "How Do You Like It Now, Gentlemen?" In *Reporting Always: Writings from the* New Yorker, 51–77. Scribner, 2015.

Salerno, Shane, and David Shields. *Salinger*. Simon and Schuster, 2014.

Sanford, Marcelline Hemingway. *At the Hemingways: With Fifty Years of Correspondence between Ernest and Marcelline Hemingway*. University of Idaho Press, 1999.

Seals, Marc. "Trauma Theory and Hemingway's Lost Paris Manuscripts." In *Hemingway: Eight Decades of Criticism*, edited by Linda Wagner-Martin, 75–87. Michigan State University Press, 2009.

SI Staff. "Double Image of a Champion." *Sports Illustrated*, December 4, 1961. https://vault.si.com/vault/1961/12/04/double-image-of-a-champion.

Slawenski, Kenneth. *J. D. Salinger*. Random House, 2012.

Spaltro, Kathleen. "Touchstone for Character: Dos Passos, Hemingway, Welles, and 'The Spanish Earth.'" *Wellesnet*, February 14, 2019. https://www.wellesnet.com/passos-hemingway-welles-spanish-earth.

Spanier, Sandra. "Finding Marlene Dietrich: An Object Lesson." *Hemingway Review* 40, no. 1 (Fall 2020): 93–95.

Spencer, Luke J. "Hemingway's Last Penny." *Atlas Obscura*, February 17, 2014. https://www.atlasobscura.com/places/hemingway-s-last -penny.

Stafford, Edward. "An Afternoon with Hemingway." *Writer's Digest*, [1964] March 11, 2008. https://www.writersdigest.com/literary -fiction-by-writing-genre/an-interview-with-hemingway.

Stańska, Zuzanna. "The Old Man and the Art: Ernest Hemingway's Art Collection." *DailyArt Magazine*, August 5, 2016. https://www .dailyartmagazine.com/ernest-hemingways-art-collection.

Stevens, Wallace. "The Idea of Order at Key West." *Collected Poetry & Prose*, edited by Frank Kermode and Joan Richardson. Library of America, 1997, 105–6.

Thomson, David. *Rosebud: The Story of Orson Welles*. Vintage, 1997.

Trogdon, Robert. "'I Am Constructing a Legend': Ernest Hemingway in Guy Hickok's *Brooklyn Daily Eagle* Articles." *Resources for American Literary Study* 37 (January 2014): 181–207.

Trouard, Dawn. "The Last Safari." *Washington Post*, June 27, 1999, https://www.washingtonpost.com/archive/entertainment/books/ 1999/06/27/the-last-safari/e0cf050f-1c69-428c-9284-b3188f815 a25.

Vaill, Amanda. *Everybody Was So Young: Gerald and Sara Murphy—A Lost Generation Love Story*. Crown, 1999.

———. *Hotel Florida: Truth, Love, and Death in the Spanish Civil War*. Picador, 2015.

Villarreal, René, and Raúl Villarreal. *Hemingway's Cuban Son: Reflections on the Writer by his Longtime Majordomo*. Kent State University Press, 2008.

Warczak, Katie. "When Dietrich Met Hemingway: Archival Documents Correct the Biographical Record." *Hemingway Review* 40, no. 1 (Fall 2020): 96–103.

"We Are All Broken. That's How the Light Gets In." Quote Investigator, November 16, 2016, https://quoteinvestigator.com/2016/11/16/light.

Welles, Orson. "Interview with Michael Parkinson (BBC 1974)." YouTube, uploaded by FilmKunst, June 29, 2013. https://youtu.be/6dAGcorF1Vo.

———, and Peter Bogdanovich. *This is Orson Welles*. Da Capo, 1998.

Wheeler, Robert. *Hemingway's Havana: A Reflection of the Writer's Life in Cuba*. Skyhorse, 2018.

"Write Drunk, Revise Sober." Quote Investigator, September 21, 2016. https://quoteinvestigator.com/2016/09/21/write-drunk.

"Writing Is Easy; You Just Open a Vein and Bleed." Quote Investigator, September 11, 2011. https://quoteinvestigator.com/2011/09/14/writing-bleed.

Yalom, Irving. *Momma and the Meaning of Life: Tales from Psychotherapy*. Basic Books, 2014.

Young, Philip. *Ernest Hemingway: A Reconsideration*. Pennsylvania State University Press, [1966] 1981.

Zaffaris, Jess. "Did Hemingway Say 'Write Drunk, Edit Sober'? Nope—He Preferred to Write Sober." *Writer's Digest*, December 20, 2018. https://www.writersdigest.com/be-inspired/did-hemingway-say-write-drunk-edit-sober-nope-he-preferred-to-write-sober.

Zeck, Melanie. "Josephine Baker, the Most Sensational Woman Anybody Ever Saw." *Oxford University Press Blog*, June 3, 2014. https://blog.oup.com/2014/06/josephine-baker-sensational-woman.

INDEX

Note: "EH" refers to Ernest Hemingway.